Gamification with Unity 5.x

Build exhilarating gaming experiences using a wide range of
game elements in Unity 5.x

Lauren S. Ferro

BIRMINGHAM - MUMBAI

Gamification with Unity 5.x

Copyright © 2016 Packt Publishing

First published: November 2016

Production reference: 1231116

Published by Packt Publishing Ltd.
Livery Place
35 Livery Street
Birmingham
B3 2PB, UK.
ISBN 978-1-78646-348-7

www.packtpub.com

Credits

Author

Lauren S. Ferro

Reviewer

Charles Palmer

Commissioning Editor

Amarabha Banerjee

Acquisition Editor

Larissa Pinto

Content Development Editor

Sachin Karnani

Technical Editor

Sachit Bedi

Copy Editor

Safis Editing

Project Coordinator

Ritika Manoj

Proofreader

Safis Editing

Indexer

Rekha Nair

Graphics

Abhinash Sahu

Production Coordinator

Melwyn Dsa

About the Author

Lauren S. Ferro is a gamification consultant and designer of game and game-like applications. She has worked, designed, consulted, and implemented strategies for a range of different purposes, including professional development, recommendation systems, and educational games. She is an active researcher in the area of gamification, player profiling, and user-centered game design. Lauren runs workshops both for the general public and companies that focus on designing user-centered games and game-like applications. She is also the creator of a game design resource, Gamicards, which is a prototyping tool for both games and game-like experiences, which is centered on player's preferences for game elements and mechanics.

She is passionate about the future of games and the technologies surrounding them, as well as their potential to improve the lives people.

When she is not playing or creating games, you can find her flying kites, creating music, or whipping up a storm in the kitchen.

Whether directly or indirectly, it takes a combined effort to create something wonderful. For this reason, I would like to thank the following for their contributions towards the development and completion of this book: Packt Publishing and everyone involved in publication of this book. Thank you for providing me with the opportunity to write about gamification. It has been a fantastic journey and I have enjoyed being a part of the community. In particular, I would like to thank Sachin Karnani for his help through the development of this book. Your comments, suggestions, and edits through each stage have helped to make this book great. The reviewers who have taken the time to read this book and provide suggestions and feedback to improve it for the future readers. Francesco Sapio, for his help and support throughout the process of writing this book. His knowledge, experience and expertise has been more than valuable. My parents, who have done everything to support me and for always believing in me. Thank you for being my inspiration and motivation in life, and the reason that I entered into the world of games. Lastly, to you, the reader. Thank you for entering the world of gaming, and allowing me the opportunity to provide you with information and resources that will take you on many adventures in creating your own gaming experiences. Don't just be a gamer, be a game changer.

About the Reviewer

Charles Palmer is a faculty member and administrator at Harrisburg University of Science and Technology, a STEM-focused, private, four-year comprehensive university dedicated to ensuring institutional access for underrepresented students and linking learning and research to practical outcomes.

As the Executive Director of the Center for Advanced Entertainment and Learning Technologies, Professor Palmer oversees the design and development of ventures in new and emerging technologies, serves as Program Lead for the undergraduate Interactive Media program, is an adviser to the Learning Technology Masters of Science program, coordinates a high school video game academy, and mentors university students on research projects in the fields of augmented/virtual reality, mobile computing, web application development, digital media, and interactive games.

As a technologist and public speaker, Charles uses virtual reality, 3D printing, gamification, interactive storytelling, social media, and simulations to discuss how training and performance can be improved with the inclusion of the latest technological advances.

Professor Palmer is also a co-author of the recently released *Alternate Reality Games: Gamification for Performance*, available from CRC Press and Amazon.

www.PacktPub.com

For support files and downloads related to your book, please visit www.PacktPub.com.

Did you know that Packt offers eBook versions of every book published, with PDF and ePub files available? You can upgrade to the eBook version at www.PacktPub.com and as a print book customer, you are entitled to a discount on the eBook copy. Get in touch with us at service@packtpub.com for more details.

At www.PacktPub.com, you can also read a collection of free technical articles, sign up for a range of free newsletters and receive exclusive discounts and offers on Packt books and eBooks.

https://www.packtpub.com/mapt

Get the most in-demand software skills with Mapt. Mapt gives you full access to all Packt books and video courses, as well as industry-leading tools to help you plan your personal development and advance your career.

Why subscribe?

- Fully searchable across every book published by Packt
- Copy and paste, print, and bookmark content
- On demand and accessible via a web browser

Table of Contents

Preface

As you can guess from the title of the book, this book is designed to teach you about implementing gamification into Unity. However, this isn't any ordinary how-to guide. It will give you not only a strong theoretical foundation of what gamification is, but also how it can be implemented to achieve different results. It discusses motivation, reward schedules, feedback loops, and how these all impact the end user. In addition, this book will also guide you through the process of game development from concept to implementation, including testing, iterating, marketing, and finally publishing.

What this book covers

Chapter 1, *The Anatomy of Games*, explains the different components of gameplay and their functionalities. We will explore what games are made up of–the atoms of gaming experiences and how they are used.

Chapter 2, *Who or What am I? - Understanding the Player*, tells the readers that in designing and developing a gamified application, it's very important to study and understand the audience, and how they behave as players. Therefore, in this chapter, the reader will be provided with different tools to specifically engage his target audience. More importantly, the readers will learn how to understand and to design these specific tools inside Unity.

Chapter 3, *An Engaged Player is a Happy Player*, will discuss ways to provide feedback and reinforcement as well as tracking the progress of the player during their engagement with the application. In addition, it will describe ways to actively engage players throughout the experience.

Chapter 4, *An Organized Chaos - Getting Ideas Out of Your Head and on to Paper*, will explain how to design a gamified application before starting to create a final version. The reader will learn different and specific techniques for process of creating gamified applications in different contexts, allowing the reader to have more tools to face the challenge. Furthermore, it is also shown how it is possible to use Unity during the process to help the reader to create helpful tools in Unity to generate new ideas.

Chapter 5, *Sculpting the Conceptual Beast*, shows that having a hard copy of the application the reader has in mind can avoid many restructuring and recording later. Therefore, this chapter introduces a series of tools to the reader for creating a physical prototype of the application. At this stage, the reader will get an idea of how to test it with its target audience to avoid wasting time and programming resources later on in the process. This will also extend what the reader has done in previous chapters, but add more functionality.

Chapter 6, *Breathing Life to Your First Creation: Creating and Importing Assets for Your Application!*, will show the reader how to gather all the concepts from the previous chapter and get them working together inside Unity. By the end of this chapter the reader will have acquired the right skills to implement all of them inside Unity.

Chapter 7, *Get Your Motor Running*, will explain to the reader how to implement various game elements into Unity that relate to the project. This provides the basic foundation and practical skills that the reader will need later on when developing the project. Each game element will be provided with a clear explanation of how to create it within Unity.

Chapter 8, *Break, Destroy, and Rebuild - The Art of Playtesting and Iteration*, will reveal methods of playtesting and iteration, in order to improve the design of their project. It will suggest ways to test, what to look for and what to pay attention to during this stage.

Chapter 9, *Graduating Your Project to Completion*, will wrap up everything that we have done as part of the project. It will make sure that the project is ready to publish and that the reader has developed all the necessary skills to get it to the final stage. It will also discuss different marketing techniques and approaches to online social networking services to give a gamified application the best possible chance for success across a wide audience.

Chapter 10, *Being the Best That You Can Be!*, will consider everything together that the reader has learned during the process and make recommendations some of the best practices during the design process and some of the key things to look for.

What you need for this book

Throughout the book we have used Unity 5.x to develop the gamified application. We have also used Adobe Illustrator to complete some of the images. However, it is possible to use any graphics creation program that you feel comfortable with using. In some instances, word processing software is required to create documents, but feel free to use whatever you prefer (for example, Microsoft Word, Adobe InDesign, Open Office). Other than that, the only requirement from you is to bring your imagination and creativity.

Who this book is for

If you are a project manager, game developer, or programmer who wants to create successful end-to-end gamification projects from scratch, then this is the book for you. You do not need any previous experience of working with Unity 5.X. All the details required to make the most of gamifying your projects are provided in the book.

Conventions

In this book, you will find a number of text styles that distinguish between different kinds of information. Here are some examples of these styles and an explanation of their meaning.

Code words in text, database table names, folder names, filenames, file extensions, pathnames, dummy URLs, user input, and Twitter handles are shown as follows: "Mount the downloaded `WebStorm-10*.dmg` disk image file as another disk in your system."

A block of code is set as follows:

```
using UnityEngine;
using System.Collections;
public class BrainstormingTool : MonoBehaviour {
```

New terms and **important words** are shown in bold. Words that you see on the screen, for example, in menus or dialog boxes, appear in the text like this: "They need to be inside a folder named Editor."

Warnings or important notes appear in a box like this.

Tips and tricks appear like this.

Reader feedback

Feedback from our readers is always welcome. Let us know what you think about this book-what you liked or disliked. Reader feedback is important for us as it helps us develop titles that you will really get the most out of. To send us general feedback, simply e-mail feedback@packtpub.com, and mention the book's title in the subject of your message. If there is a topic that you have expertise in and you are interested in either writing or contributing to a book, see our author guide at www.packtpub.com/authors.

Customer support

Now that you are the proud owner of a Packt book, we have a number of things to help you to get the most from your purchase.

Downloading the example code

You can download the example code files for this book from your account at http://www.packtpub.com. If you purchased this book elsewhere, you can visit http://www.packtpub.com/supportand register to have the files e-mailed directly to you.

You can download the code files by following these steps:

1. Log in or register to our website using your e-mail address and password.
2. Hover the mouse pointer on the **SUPPORT** tab at the top.
3. Click on **Code Downloads & Errata**.

4. Enter the name of the book in the **Search** box.
5. Select the book for which you're looking to download the code files.
6. Choose from the drop-down menu where you purchased this book from.
7. Click on **Code Download**.

Once the file is downloaded, please make sure that you unzip or extract the folder using the latest version of:

- WinRAR / 7-Zip for Windows
- Zipeg / iZip / UnRarX for Mac
- 7-Zip / PeaZip for Linux

The code bundle for the book is also hosted on GitHub at `https://github.com/PacktPubl ishing/Gamification-with-Unity-5x`. We also have other code bundles from our rich catalog of books and videos available at `https://github.com/PacktPublishing/`. Check them out!

Downloading the color images of this book

We also provide you with a PDF file that has color images of the screenshots/diagrams used in this book. The color images will help you better understand the changes in the output. You can download this file from `https://www.packtpub.com/sites/default/files/down loads/GamificationwithUnity5x_ColorImages.pdf`.

Errata

Although we have taken every care to ensure the accuracy of our content, mistakes do happen. If you find a mistake in one of our books-maybe a mistake in the text or the code-we would be grateful if you could report this to us. By doing so, you can save other readers from frustration and help us improve subsequent versions of this book. If you find any errata, please report them by visiting `http://www.packtpub.com/submit-errata`, selecting your book, clicking on the **Errata Submission Form** link, and entering the details of your errata. Once your errata are verified, your submission will be accepted and the errata will be uploaded to our website or added to any list of existing errata under the Errata section of that title.

To view the previously submitted errata, go to `https://www.packtpub.com/books/conten t/support`and enter the name of the book in the search field. The required information will appear under the **Errata** section.

Piracy

Piracy of copyrighted material on the Internet is an ongoing problem across all media. At Packt, we take the protection of our copyright and licenses very seriously. If you come across any illegal copies of our works in any form on the Internet, please provide us with the location address or website name immediately so that we can pursue a remedy.

Please contact us at `copyright@packtpub.com` with a link to the suspected pirated material.

We appreciate your help in protecting our authors and our ability to bring you valuable content.

Questions

If you have a problem with any aspect of this book, you can contact us at `questions@packtpub.com`, and we will do our best to address the problem.

1
The Anatomy of Games

In a world full of work, chores, and just plain boring things, we all must find the time to play. We must allow ourselves to be immerse ourselves within enchanted worlds of fantasy, to explore far-away and uncharted exotic islands throughout mysterious worlds. We may also find hidden treasure while confronting and overcoming some of our worst fears. As we enter utopian and dystopian worlds, mesmerized by the magic of games, we realize anything and everything is possible, and all that we have to do is imagine.

There are many things that are involved in creating this magical places, and in this chapter, we will begin by exploring the following:

- To begin *Not just pixels and programming* will cover the basics of what games are and the types of game that exist. It will discuss how games have developed and how to think about what a game really is.

- Next, *Playing to learn* discusses the difference types of game and gamified experiences that can have, and have had, an impact on our daily lives.

- Then, *Gamify all the things with gamification* has examples of gamified applications that are used in everyday life. It discusses the types of game element and mechanics that are used within each one, and how they encourage different types of interaction.

- To answer the question of *What is game design?* this section will explore the different kinds of element and mechanics that games and gamified experiences have.

- This chapter will conclude with, *Competency and complacency – where do we draw the line?* This section looks at how games and their components are used to get us up and off the couch and keep us engaged.

Not just pixels and programming

Gaming has an interesting and ancient history. It goes back as far as the ancient Egyptians with a game called Sennet. Long after the reign of the great Egyptian Kings, the ancient Greeks and Romans saw games as a way to display strength and stamina. However, as time has elapsed, games have not only developed from the marble pieces of Sennet or the glittering swords of battles, they have also adapted to changes in media: from stone to paper, and from paper to technology. We have seen the rise and development of physical games (for example, table and card games) to games that need us to physically move our characters by using our bodies and peripherals (Playstation Move, WiiMote), to interact with the game environment (Wii Sports, Heavy Rain). So now, not only do we have the ability to create 3D virtual worlds with virtual reality, we can enter their worlds as well. Just like the following image, which is from Dungeons and Dragons, games don't have to take on a digital form, they can also be physical.

Dungeons and Dragons board with figurines and dice

Finding your preferred type

Now, let's take it a step further and observe the different types of games that exist. There are games to teach, to train, to escape reality with, and games to transform ourselves. As we can see in the following image, there are tons of games that we can play, and across varying platforms as well!

Many different types of game that are available

To begin, you have your games for entertainment. They may have some other elements such as some accurate historic facts (Assassin's Creed, Civilization), but their main purpose is to entertain us. They can exist across a range of different genres from shooter (Call of Duty) to adventure (Fable) and can be played either alone (Alone in the Dark, Alan Wake, Metro 2033) or with company both near and far (Word of Warcraft, Dota 2, Guild Wars 2). Other genres include:

- **Action**: These games offer intensity of action as the primary attraction. They challenge the player in many ways, such as testing their hand-eye coordination and their ability to react to enemies.
- **Adventure**: These games can send us to magical faraway lands where majestic animals live and wealth and fortune await. They focus on story and problem solving to get from one part of the game world to another.
- **Arcade**: These games give us an experience similar to those from the past and provide us with the opportunity to kill invaders, destroy blocks, and dodge barrels as they inevitably hurl towards us. Gaming experiences are in essence diverse and there is definitely no one-size-fits-all approach to choosing them, let alone to create or design them.
- **Educational**: These games aim to teach us about real-world concepts and can complement the work that we may do in the classroom.
- **Fighting**: These games place us in the ring with an enemy, *or two,* and bring out the fighter in us. They often feature players competing against each other in a battle of strength and endurance.

- **Horror**: These games have us terrified, unable to move while our hearts are racing as we turn every corner; horror games are what nightmares are made of. They feature overwhelmed protagonist(s), an oppressive atmosphere, and a need for careful management of resources (ammo, health, and so on).
- **Massively Multiplayer Online (MMO)**: These games are just that. They are games that contain large amounts of players, from all corners of the globe, engaging in various types of gameplay. Players engage in real time and encourage social interaction. They can traverse various detailed and immersive worlds, or solve puzzles against enemies or with allies. MMO's also allow the player to engage with intricate storylines while completing various quests throughout the worlds.
- **Music/Rhythm**: These games get you into a rhythm where the player has to input the same synchronized action to a beat or melody such as singing with the right pitch or pushing buttons on a guitar in the right sequence.
- **Platformer**: These games are all about *platforming*. They require the player to jump from one edge to another; sometimes straight into enemy characters over terrifying voids, flames, or even poisonous liquid.
- **Puzzle**: These games require focus and concentration. They test your mental skills as well as your dexterity and reflexes.
- **Racing/Driving**: These games are where the player drives a vehicle of some kind and races against either other players or time. Such games may create or even break friendships (such as Mario Kart).
- **Role Playing Games (RPG's)**: RPGs allow us to live out our fantasies as other people or even species. We can be whoever we want, wherever we choose.
- **Shooters (First-Person Shooter (FPS)/Third-Person Shooter (TPS))**: These games require the player to go around as a lone agent, team, or rogue and kill anything that moves. These fast-paced games bring out the competitive element within us. We might forge strong bonds or in some cases destroy them.
- **Simulation**: These games simulate parts of a reality.
- **Sports**: These games allow you to race, swim, and fly. We can live the dream of extreme sports (without the risk) or become an athlete that inspires us.
- **Strategy**: These games require you to think outside the box; they challenge your logic and question your reasoning. It is up to you, the player, to come up with plans and tactics to overcome all the challenges that you will face.

To get a better understanding about different types of genres, try to play a few games from each, albeit on consoles, PC, or mobile. If you don't have a lot of time to spare, check out gameplay videos and see how each genre differs in gameplay.

Playing to learn

The structure of these types of game is what gameplay is molded around. Ultimately, these games aim to teach a concept (or many) to players in more interesting ways than reading the same information from a textbook. In some instances, you will have an educational game, where designers entwine the learning objectives into an abstracted reality; and then there are games that stylize reality.

Minecraft

Minecraft is an open-world sandbox type of game where the player can create basically anything that they put their mind to. Just as we can see in the following screenshot, the world of Minecraft is made up of *blocks* that the player must collect in order to create range of things from houses to the Enterprise. While this game was not necessarily designed to be used as part of a formal educational environment, just that happened. So much so in fact that some schools have integrated it into their lesson plans and curriculum. To this extent, **MinecraftEdu** which was its educational version (`https://education.minecraft.net/`), was created in 2011 so that it can better support learning objectives. The main concept for creating MinecraftEdu was so that it could preserve the world of creation that original Minecraft offered while adding elements that enabled it to be effectively used within the classroom. The use of Minecraft and MinecraftEdu has ranged from teaching math concepts to teaching languages.

In-game screenshot of Minecraft

Kerbal Space Program

Kerbal Space Program (www.kerbalspaceprogram.com) allows the player to create their own space program. This starts with the construction of a spacecraft that is not only capable of flying its crew out into space, but also doesn't kill them. In order to do this, the player has a set of different parts, which are then used to build the functional spacecraft. Each piece serves its own function and will affect the way that the spacecraft flies (or doesn't, just like in the following screenshot). Furthermore, the game supports different game modes. For instance, in the Career Mode, the player has the possibility to expand and manage their own Space Center, by completing missions and researching new technologies. Another is the Sandbox mode, where the player can explore the Kerbal universe without restrictions. Finally, the Science mode is a mix between the previous two.

In-game screenshot of Kerbal Space Program with a crashed spaceship

Sid Meier's Civilization

Imagine being Montezuma of the Aztecs, Darius I of Persia, or Augustus Caesar of Rome like in the following screenshot. Can you image taking the role of some of the most famous historical people that we have only read about? Not only this, but also being the person who must guide the development of a civilization from the first settlements, through the bronze and golden ages all the way through the industrial revolution; and then end up putting a man on the moon, whilst maintaining relationships with nearby nations. Simple...*right*?

In-game screenshot of Augustus Caesar displaying the background history to the player before they embark on creating their own civilization

Sid Meier's Civilization (1991-2016) series are prime examples of how the natural progression of history plays out depending on how the communities develop skills and infrastructure. In Civilization V (www.civilization5.com) the player can take the role of a historic figure such as Napoleon Bonaparte, Augustus Caesar, or Alexander the Great. The player learns about the history behind each of these great leaders and the time in which they held reign over their respective countries and civilizations. However, what needs to be noted is that the player does not take the explicit role of the historical figure, as they play during different historical periods. The player is effectively writing history as a historical character. In this way, it's possible for Augustus Caesar to order the construction of the pyramids of Giza. This sets up the premise for competitive gameplay among systems within the game and among the gaming community. To get their civilization further along quicker, the player needs to utilize the game's systems more effectively.

It is during historic periods of time (for example, golden age, bronze age, and so on) that the player finds out how their actions affect the outcome of the civilization and the choices resulting in progression and outcomes that allow the player to create an understanding about how different actions and solutions affect the development of a civilization.

Stop kidding around, be serious!

Serious games take concepts from reality that we need to learn, and stylize them in a way that is similar to reality. Whether we are learning about running our own business or a new language, the way that we receive information does not need to remain in endless pages of large textbooks or involves copying notes from classroom whiteboards. The monotonous method of learning can be changed, and serious games take this information and present it as part of an immersive and interactive e-learning environment. Fortunately enough, serious games also provide the ability to test out the knowledge that we learn along the way.

America's Army

The game is a FPS published in 2002 by the U.S. Army (www.americasarmy.com) and is branded as a strategic communication device, designed to allow young Americans to virtually explore the Army at their own pace. The game was created to identify player's interests and then to determine if it matches their needs, interests, and abilities with a view to being part of the U.S. Army. In fact, America's Army represents the first large-scale use of game technology by the U.S. government as a platform for strategic communication and the first use of game technology in support of U.S. Army recruiting.

Screenshot of two different environments from America's Army

Foldit

Foldit (www.fold.it) is an online game that is part of an experimental research project developed by the University of Washington's Center for Game Science in collaboration with the UW Department of Biochemistry. Players are required to fold the structures of selected proteins using tools that are provided in the game. We can see an example of how the player learns how such structures are formed, in the following image. Of all the solutions, those that score the highest are then analyzed by researchers, who then determine whether there is a native structural configuration (native state) that can be applied to relevant proteins in the real world. What is useful about Foldit is that scientists can then use these solutions to target, eradicate diseases, and create biological innovations. Some of the many successful case stories include www.scientificamerican.com/article/foldit-gamers-solve-riddle and http://www.nature.com/articles/ncomms12549. You are also encouraged to explore other success stories and news surrounding Foldit.

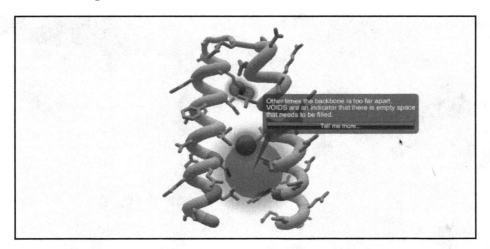

In-game screenshot of a tutorial part of Foldit

Moonbase Alpha

NASA has once again landed on the moon; however, this time their aim is to colonize, research, and further their exploration. After arriving on the Lunar surface, NASA established a small outpost on the south pole of the moon called Moonbase Alpha (www.nasa.gov/moonbasealpha). Not long after establishing the Moonbase, it became self-sufficient and plans for further expansion were begun.

In Moonbase Alpha, you are an astronaut working to further human expansion and research. However, upon returning from a research expedition, you witness a meteorite impact that cripples the life support capability of the newly established base. With time ticking away with each passing moment, it is up to you and your team to repair (as seen in the following screenshot) and replace equipment in order to restore the oxygen production to the settlement and survive.

Moonbase Alpha requires team coordination along with the use and allocation of your available resources such as robots, rovers, repair tools, and so on. These resources are key to you and your team's overall success and survival. There are several ways that the life support system of the lunar base can be restored. However, you are pressed for time and must work efficiently and effectively, learn from decisions (both good and bad), which are taken in previous gaming sessions. Ultimately, this learning process provides the much needed insight to rise above others on the leaderboard and come out as the ideal astronaut to save you and your team from imminent death in the dark depths of space.

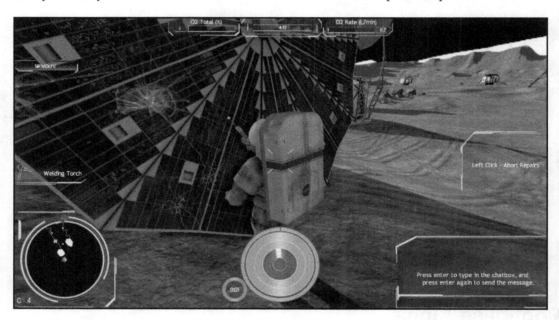

In-game screenshot of the player's avatar (the astronaut) repairing a broken part of the space station

Keeping it real with simulations

Next, there are games that try to emulate reality. These are simulations and they simulate real-world consequences. For example, if you die, you have to start again. They can exist in both fantasy and realistic worlds, but just like real life their consequences are permanent.

Virtual Heroes

Virtual Heroes (www.virtualheroes.com) specializes in 3D simulations that are aimed predominantly towards medical or military training. These are two areas where accurate decisions and fast action can be the difference between living and dying. In reality, it can be dangerous to engage in real scenarios due to the risks that they contain. As a result, it is nearly impossible for new trainees to practice in real-life contexts, and get the much needed skills before heading out on the job. Thankfully, 3D simulated environments (such as those that we can see in the following screenshot) in Virtual Heroes not only offer the space to practice essential skills, but also an environment that contains a higher level of safety where novice personnel can perform various tasks without putting anyone at risk. For example, in emergency room situations, patients are able to interact in simulated scenarios. This process allows for failure, where the student can learn from their mistakes without endangering actual patients. From these experiences, students can be trained to think quickly and make appropriate decisions. As the students progress and develop their skills, the scenarios can be modified so that they present new challenges that offer more opportunities to practice and use the previously developed skills. On the backend of these programs, data can be collected, which can provide insights in to how well or badly students perform. As a result, instructors are able to identify problematic areas that will then help to inform them about what areas to focus on when designing future tasks.

In-game screenshot from Virtual Heroes displaying two different types of environment and situation that a player can face during the game

SimCity

SimCity (www.simcity.com) is a rare example of a long-term multiplayer simulation game. In all the other games of the same series, the player has to manage a city. In SimCity, the player controls an entire region that could contain up to 16 cities with different specializations that the player has to control at the same time. Also, they have the possibility to interact with other players' cities. Both a collaborative or competitive behavior can be adopted by the player to guide them during the decision making process. There are no right or wrong choices, but all of them have consequences. For example, building a casino will bring tourists, and therefore money as well, but it will encourage criminal activity. As a result, your city will become more dangerous and it may ultimately affect your population levels. In addition, universities can research new technologies, but they are very expensive to maintain in comparison to other types of buildings and facilities.

If we look at the following image of SimCity, we can get a feel for many aspects that the player will need to learn, just by the HUD alone! From keeping the citizens happy, managing economies, and building infrastructure, lessons can be learnt, which can then be adapted to real life from such experiences.

Screenshot during gameplay of SimCity

From Dust

From Dust (`www.ubisoft.com/en-GB/game/from-dust`) recreates the world and the story of a primitive tribe that fights to survive in a hostile environment, in constant evolution. The player has to control the elements to keep their people safe from tsunamis, wildfires, earthquakes, volcanoes, and torrential rains. As we can see in the following screenshot, players begin with building the most basic of things such as bridges to provide a means of getting from one part of the map to the other. The only way to survive is to investigate the ancestors to restore a lost power. Furthermore, the game comes with different modes that the player can be challenged on, from puzzle-based modes to time modes with a lot of pressure. Finally, the game also provides a way to share the player's result in a general leaderboard and let them join a special community.

Screenshot taken during the tutorial level in From Dust

Gamify all things with gamification

Lastly, we have gamified experiences. The aim of these experiences is to improve something about ourselves in ways that are ideally more motivating than how we perceive them in real life. For example, think of something that you find difficult to stay motivated with. This may be anything from managing your finances, learning a new language, or even exercising.

Now, if you make a deal with yourself to buy a new dress once you finished managing your finances or to go on a trip once you have learned a new language, you are turning the experience into a game. The rules are simply to finish the task, and the condition of finishing it results in a reward, either a dress or the trip. The fundamental thing to remember is that gamified experiences aim to make ordinary tasks extraordinary and enjoyable for the player.

Games, gaming, and gamified experiences can give rise to many types of opportunities for us to play or even escape reality. To finish this brief exploration into the design of games, we must realize that games are not solely about sitting in front of the TV, playing on the computer, or being glued to the seat transfixed by a digital character dodging bullets. The game mechanics to make a task more engaging and fun have been defined as *Gamification*. Gamification relates to the use of games to tackle issues related to real-world situations, and while the term has become popular, the concept is not entirely new. Think about loyalty cards, not just frequent flyer mile programs, but maybe even at your local butcher or café. Do you get a discount after a certain number of purchases; maybe the 10th coffee is free. For a while, various reward schemes have already been in place; even giving children a reward for completing household chores or good behavior and awarding *gold stars* for academic excellence constitute gamification. If you consider social activities such as Scouts, they utilize *gamification* as part of their procedures. Scouts learn new skills, such as cooperativeness, and by doing so gain different status, and receive badges to demonstrate levels of competency. Gamification has become a favorable approach to *engaging* clients with new and exciting design schemes to maintain interest and promote a more enjoyable and ideally "*fun*" product. The product in question does not have to be *digital*. Therefore, *gamification* can exist both in a physical realm (as mentioned before with gold stars awards) as well as in a more prominent digital sense (such as badge and point reward systems) as an effective way to motivate and engage users. Some common examples of gamification include:

- **Loyalty programs**: Each time you engage with the company in a particular way such as buying certain products, *or amount of* you are rewarded. These rewards can include additional products, points towards items, discounts, and even free items.
- **School House points**: A pastime that some of us may remember, especially for fans of Harry Potter. Each time you do the right thing such as following the school rules you get some points. Alternatively, you do the wrong thing and you lose points.
- **Scouts**: They reward levels of competency with badges as well as ranks. The more skilled you are the more badges you collect, wear, and ultimately the faster you work your way up the hierarchy.

- **Rewarding in general**: This will often be associated with some rules and these rules determine whether or not a reward is obtained. Eat your vegetables, you get dessert; do you math homework you get to play. Both have winning conditions.
- **Tests**: As horrifying as it might sound they can be considered as a game. For example, we're on a quest to learn about history. Each assignment you get is like a task, preparing you for the final battle...*the exam*. At the end of all these assessments, you get a score or a grade that indicates to you your progress as you pass from one concept to the next. Ultimately, your final exam will determine your rank among your peers and whether or not you make it to the next level or not (that being anywhere from your year level to a university). It may be also worth noting that just like in games, you also have those trying to work the system, searching for glitches in the system that they can exploit. However, just like games, they too eventually are kicked.

Language learning with DuoLingo

DuoLingo (www.duolingo.com) is an interesting application in terms of its design. It is a simple yet powerful tool for grasping foundational concepts in a range of different languages. DuoLingo has quite a fresh color palette and it immediately grabs the attention of the user with its bold and simple graphics. If we have a look at the following screenshot, we can see that the content is contained in small chunks (for example, basic vocabulary, food) and each lesson focuses on a small section of each part. This works well because it doesn't become too overwhelming to the player.

Various screenshots displaying different parts of the DuoLingo application

Game elements and mechanics

DuoLingo includes a number of different game elements and of course they are used in varying ways. The following is a list of the game elements that are used as part of the DuoLingo application and how they are used:

- **Badges**: These are used in DuoLingo as a way to identify each new concept to be learnt. Each badge is representative of a certain topic, for example, hamburger for food, conversation bubbles for phrases, and so on.
- **Progress Bars**: These are used in a number of ways to indicate both progress as a whole as you complete lessons, and progress within the lessons themselves. As the bars fill, the retention of words is at their highest. However, the bars begin to decline if a user doesn't revise the newly learnt content for each category. The main difference between badges and progress bars is that badges represent completed tasks and progress bars are used to indicate to the player how far they have come and how far they still have to go.
- **Leaderboards**: They are implemented for users to compete against one another.
- **Currency**: This is used in DuoLingo with *Lingots*. Lingots are the virtual currency of DuoLingo, which you can obtain when you complete certain tasks within the game.
- **Experience points**: These are used to indicate to the player how well they are doing. Each time they practice previously learnt content, they earn experience points. They can keep track of their experience points over the week by observing a graph and even progress bars within each topic.
- **Unlockables**: These are featured in two different ways. The first way is by completing previous topics (such as adverbs, tenses, and so on) as well as parts of topics. The second is by using Lingots to obtain items that are unavailable until the user has enough to purchase the items in the store.
- **Countdowns**: These are used in DuoLingo to test the speed of a user who has completed a module. In one way, it encourages the player to compete against themselves to not only beat the timer, but to also do better than the other previous attempts by obtaining a faster time.
- **Lives**: In the timed mode, a player has in total three lives that allow them to answer a question incorrectly. Once they have run out of lives they must start again.

Becoming a better human with Habitica (HabitRPG)

Real life can be mundane in some parts, especially when we are trying to keep on top of to-do lists, or develop better habits. However, don't worry, Habitica is one gamified application that adds a bit of drama to whatever new habit you are trying to develop (or stop). As we can see in the following image, Habitica has a dashboard as its main interface. All the information is displayed to the player at a glance, and more specific information, such as daily tasks and chats, is displayed in other, yet easily accessible, parts.

Screenshot of the rewards section of Habitica

Game elements and mechanics

Like DuoLingo, it uses similar elements and some new ones to achieve different things. The following is a list of game elements that are found in Habitica and how they are used as part of the gaming experience:

- **Levels**: These are featured with the player advancing as they gain experience points and retain lives.
- **Progress Bars**: These feature a lot throughout Habitica, representing many different parts. For example, progress bars represent the amount of experience as well as mana (to fight against various creatures).
- **Status**: These levels differentiate the types of classes for player and the abilities that they have against creatures.
- **Lives**: These are the number of lives that a player has remaining against creatures within the game. Each time a player does not complete a daily task or habit on time, they lose some life points.
- **Experience Points**: They are for each player and are associated with successfully completing tasks and habits. With each successful check-in, a player gains a small amount of experience towards leveling their character up.

Shop till you drop with AliExpress (mobile application)

While we many not necessarily need an excuse to shop, because let's face it we can *always* buy ourselves something, AliExpress (www.aliexpress.com) has turned part of its service into a game with their mobile application. To encourage users to download, install, and use their application a number of games and exclusive offers have been designed to offer savings and some items for *almost* free (+ $0.01 for shipping), if you are lucky enough to grab them in time. As we can see in the following screenshot, Ali Express keeps a log of the user's interactions, for example, how successful or unsuccessful they have been with daily spins.

In addition, the user is also rewarded with feedback when good things happen, such as winning coins from spinning the wheel.

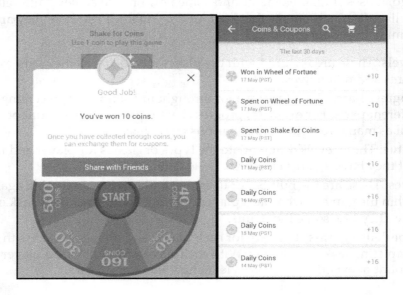

Screenshot of various elements from Ali Express that encourage the user to engage with gamified elements such as spining the Wheel and collecting daily coins.

Game elements and mechanics

Ali Express is slightly different from both DuoLingo and Habitica; it's an application for purchasing goods, rather than curving a spending habit or learning Italian. The following is a list of how various game elements are used to engage the user:

- **Points**: These are used in a number of ways with AliExpress. For example, they are associated with different actions. For the most part, points indicate to the user how well they are doing overall in terms of submitting feedback to buyers and receiving feedback from sellers.
  Feedback is also associated with points. Each time a user gives and receives feedback they are provided with points that are then attributed to a level.
- **Badges**: These are usually included during special events and require that a user complete certain tasks, such as adding an item to their wishlist, to get the *daily* badge.
- **Levels**: These indicate the user's interaction with the application. For example, since giving and providing feedback allows them to level up, reaching a new level provides additional rewards. For example, they may have the ability to be

notified in advanced about upcoming sales and receive extra discounts.

- **Progress Bars**: These are used to track the number of points that you have accumulated towards each level. Points that contribute to the overall progress are related to providing feedback for purchases, buying items, and daily shopping.
- **Virtual Currency**: This is used in the way of coins. Coins allow users to buy various items (if they are quick enough!) and exchange coupons that give them discounts off their next purchases.
- **Mini-games**: *Spin the wheel and Shake* is one of a few mini-games that users have the chance to engage with. The game provide users with the ability to win additional coins to buy better items with or greater discount coupons.
- **Chance**: This provides users with a feeling of mystery, especially if they are playing mini-games. It is enticing, with each spin of the wheel or shake of the phone having the possibility to result in a large amount of coins.
- **Unlockables**: These are used for giving access to different features such as fast refunds, fast track claims, and price cut notifications.

What is game design?

So, as we have discussed, many types of game exist and therefore design approach. There are different ways that you can design, implement, and create games. Now, let's take a brief look at *how* games are made and more importantly, *what* they are made of:

1. *Generating ideas* involves thinking about the story that we want to tell, or a trip that we may take the player on. At this stage, we're just getting everything out of our head and onto paper. Everything and anything should be written, the stranger and more abstract the idea, the better. It is important at this stage not to feel trapped by thinking an idea may not be *suitable*. Often, the first few ideas that we create are the worst, and the great stuff comes from iterating all the ideas that we put down in this stage. Talk about your ideas with friends, family, even online forums are a great place to get feedback on your initial concepts. One of the first things that any aspiring game designer can begin with is looking at what is already out there. A lot is learnt when we succeed, or fail, especially why and how. Therefore, at this stage, you will want to do a bit of research about what you are designing. For instance, if you're designing an application to teach English, not only should you see what other applications exist, but also how English is actually taught, even in an educational environment. It doesn't have to stop there either. Observing how games *teach* ideas and concepts can also provide you with ideas to implement into your own gamified application.

While you are generating ideas, it is also useful to think about the technology and materials that you will use along the way. What game engine is better for your game's direction? Do you need to purchase licenses if you are intending to make your game commercial? Answering these kinds of questions earlier on can save many headaches later on when you have your concept ready to go, especially if you need to learn *how to use* the software as some have steep learning curves.

2. *Defining your idea* is not just a beautiful piece of art that we see when a game is being created. It can be rough, messy, and downright simple, but it communicates the idea. It might even be worthwhile to show an example of the process from other games, such as the initial sketch of an object, its iterations, and then its final outcome. Not just this, it also communicates the design of the game's space and how a player may interact and even traverse it. Concept design is an art in itself and includes concepts on environments, characters puzzles, and even the quest itself. We take the ideas that we had during the idea generation and we *flesh them out*. We begin to refine them, to see what works and what doesn't. Again, at this stage it is important to get feedback. The importance of feedback is vital. When we are designing games, we often are caught up, we are so immersed in our ideas, and to us they make sense. We have sorted out every detail (at least for the most part it feels like that). However, you aren't designing for you, you are designing for your audience and getting an outsider's opinion can be crucial and even offer a perspective that you might not necessarily have thought of. This stage also includes the story. Life without existence is like a game without a story. What kind of story do you want your player to be a part of? Can they control it, or is it set in stone? Who are the characters? The answers to these questions breathe soul into your ideas. While you are designing your story, keep referring to the concept that you have created, the atmosphere, the characters, and the type of environment that you envision. Some other aspects of your game that you will need to consider at this stage are:

   - How will your players learn how to play your game?
   - How will the game progress? This may include introducing different abilities, challenges, levels, and so on. Here is where you will need to observe the flow of the game. Too much happening and you have a recipe for chaos, not enough and your player will get bored.
   - Number of players that you envision playing your game (even if you intend for a **co-op** or online mode).

- What are the main features that will be in your game?
- How will you market your game? Will there be an online blog that documents the stages of development? Will it include interviews with different members of the team? Will there be different content that is tailored for each network (such as Twitter, Facebook, Instagram, and so on)?

3. *Bringing it together* is thinking about how all your ideas come together and how they work, or don't. Think of this stage like creating a painting. You may have all the pieces, but you need to know how to use them to create the piece of art. Some brushes (such as story and characters) work better with other paints (for example, game elements, mechanics, and so on). This stage is about bringing your ideas and concepts into reality. This stage features design processes such as:
    - Storyboards, which give an overview of how the story and gameplay evolve throughout the game.
    - Character design sheets, which outline characteristics about who your characters are and how they fit into the story.
    - **Game User Interfaces** (**GUI**'s), which will provide information to the player during gameplay. This may include elements such as progress bars, points, and items that they collect along the way.

4. *Prototyping* is where things get *real*...well relatively. It may be something as simple as a piece of paper or something more complex such as a 3D model. You then begin to create the environments or the levels that your player will explore. As you develop your world, you will take your content and populate the levels. Prototyping is where we take what was in our head and sketched out on paper and use it to sculpt the gameful beast. The main purpose of this stage is to see how everything works, or *doesn't*. For example, the fantastic idea of a huge mech-warrior with flames shooting out of an enormous gun on its back was perhaps not the *fantastic* idea that it was on paper, at least not in the intended part of the game.

Rapid prototyping is fast and rough. Remember when you were in school and you had things such as glue, scissors, pens, and pencils, well that is what you will need for this. It gets the game to a functioning point before you spend tireless hours in a game engine trying to create your game. A few bad rapid prototypes early on can save a lot time than one digital one. Lastly, rapid prototyping isn't just for the preliminary prototyping phase. It can be used before you add in any new features to your game once it's already set up

5. *Iteration* is like what an iron is to a creased shirt. You want your game to be on point and iterating it gets it to that stage. For instance, that awesome mech-warrior that you created for the first level was perhaps better as the final boss. Iteration is about fine-tuning the game, tweaking it so that it not only flows better overall, but also the gameplay is improved.

6. *Playtesting* is the most important part of the whole process once you have your game at a relatively functioning level. The main concept here is to playtest, playtest, and playtest. It cannot be emphasized enough about the importance of this stage. More often than not, games are released buggy, with problems and issues that could have been avoided during this stage. As a result, players lose interest, reviews contain frustration and disappointment, which let's face it we don't want after hours and hours of blood, sweat, and tears. The key here is to not only playtest your game, but to playtest it in multiple ways, on multiple devices, with a range of different people. If you release your game on the PC, test it on a high-performance one and a low-performance one. The same process should be applied for mobile devices (phones and tablets) and operating systems! We will cover this in more detail in Chapter 8, Break, Destroy and Rebuild – The Art of Playtesting and Iteration.

7. *Evaluate* your game based on the playtesting.

 Iterating, playtesting, and evaluating are three steps that you will go through on a regular basis, more so as you implement a new feature or tweak an existing one. This cycle is important. You wouldn't buy a car that has parts added without being tested first so why should a player buy a game with untested features?

8. *Build* your game and get it ready for distribution, on CD or online as a digital download.

9. *Publish* your game! Your baby has come of age and is ready to be released out into the wild where it will be a portal for players around the world to enter the world that you (and your team) have created from scratch. The publication process will be covered in more detail in Chapter 9, *Graduating your Project to Completion*.

Conjuring the elements

Think about the fundamental components of life; we have atoms, cells, neurons; we have many things that are combined to create the structure. Games are no different. Games are like chemistry, you combine the right elements and mechanics (which we will discuss shortly) and you have the potential to cause an *impressive* reaction, a type of gameplay; of course keep in mind that it can always work in reverse!

To begin, games are made of a range of different *elements*. Elements can be considered as the *what* of game design. What does the player get for killing enemies, for completing objectives consecutively and on time? Does the player get a badge, some points, or do they level up and become higher ranked? All these things are combined to create unique experiences.

The following is a list of the basic game elements that we will discuss and cover throughout this book. In addition, this list provides you with a basic overview of some of the most popular game elements that can be found in any game:

- **Avatars** are representations of players in games. You can think of them as 2D such as an icon, or even 3D such as the actual character that you play. They can be make-believe; user-created, or even the user themselves.
- **Achievements** represent some type of accomplishment. The process of obtaining achievements may be through varying challenges of varying levels of difficulty, exploration, as with the case of hidden achievements, or locked achievements that require you to have obtained something earlier in order to unlock the achievement. In general, achievements are often built around different types of behavior.
- **Badges** are icons that you receive for doing a particular action(s) and/or completing objectives. They differ from achievements in the sense that they are usually a visual representation of achievements (or groups of them). Examples may include trophies, like on the Playstation Network.
- **Bars** (such as progress bars) indicate various factors such as health, mana, and experience levels. They can come in many shapes and forms. For example, progress bars can be segmented, they can be one continuous bar, and they can be circular, rectangular, and colored.
- **Bonuses** act as an *extra something* to contribute towards other rewards. They may come in the form of additional items, more experience, aid in completing an achievement (such as extra coins). For example, if you kill twenty enemies within 30 seconds, you get extra points as opposed to if you kill them within 30 minutes.

- **Collectables** include anything that you can and want to collect such as pens, postcards, coins, stamps, and so on. Similar things exist within games. In some cases, these items can be used, traded, or sold for other items; in other cases, they are just there for the sake of it, so you can boast to other players that you have something or a lot of something that is relatively special to the game. Many games have one-time collectables during festive times of the year such as Christmas or Halloween.

- **Combos** require the player to group items together to perform a certain behavior or obtain particular items. For example, if you're playing a fighting game such as Tekken or Street Fighter, pressing certain buttons in sequence will result in a combined attack. Combos can also include the player combining various elements together to create or obtain a greater item.

- **Countdowns/timers** are just like the days in reality that come and go, games incorporate the element of time in various ways. For example, to avoid the player idling for too long, designers may limit the amount of time that it takes a player to complete an objective. They usually push a player to improve so that the time they take to complete an objective becomes more efficient. Time limits are not necessarily used just to improve the player's efficiency, or as idle time, they can be used to increase the difficulty by giving the player less time to do something. It can also add a sense of urgency and tension to the game's atmosphere.

- **Currency** whether virtual or real currency can be used to obtain items (in the real and virtual world). In some games, such as EVE Online, actual stock markets exist that influence the price of virtual goods. Some examples of virtual currency include ISK (EVE online), Gil (Final Fantasy), Lingots (DuoLingo), and coins and gems (Clash Royale and many other casual games).

- **Difficulty** allows the user to select a level of difficulty before they engage with an experience that can increase the level of immersion. Common types of difficulty include levels of easy, medium, and hard; time constraints; limited resources such as ammunition, weapons, medical supplies, stronger and/or an increased number of enemies; and damage (for example, the amount of times that you can be shot at until you have no health left).

- **Easter Eggs** are a special secret event that a user can discover. They can be various types such as inside jokes from the developers, or even the community. Some great examples include the elevator rave in Crysis 2, the disco party in Stanley Parable, or the giant ocean bunny in Saints Row 2.

- **Feedback** provides information about the user's interaction, which is important for not only motivating the player, but to also let them know about their interaction. This can be after a particular action, duration, or series of actions and behaviors. Types of feedback can be a dialogue box on the screen saying something like *Well done!* or even an audio clip indicating a right or wrong action.

- **Items** include anything from useful objects that you receive (physical and/or digital) for performing a particular action, exploration, to additional ammunition, medical supplies, and power-ups, which can be items in games that your player can obtain, require, and eventually use. The distribution of items, their availability, and where they are located will depend on how challenging you want your experience to be as well as the reward schedule that you are planning to implement.

- **Leaderboards** are a great way of showing to the rest of the world that you are number one (or at least ranked somewhere). Your rank among other users is based on a parameter(s) such as points, achievements, kill/death ratios, and so forth. Leaderboards can be based on all-time scores; momentary ranking such as daily, weekly, and even monthly player's scores.

- **Levels** are a way of providing a sense of progress to a player. They can be in the form of varying levels of difficulty, or the strength of abilities that a player has. In addition, levels can also indicate the natural progression of the player to another location as they advance through the game. An example of levels would be progressing through different areas and locations such as those within God of War and Army of 2.

- **Permadeath** as the name suggests, the death of a character or player during gameplay is permanent. If the player wants to continue, they must start from the beginning.

- **Points** are usually numerical in value and due to a player performing an action. Points can be added or subtracted depending on what the action was. For example, if the aim is to shoot enemies the player gets a point; if on the other hand, they shoot their teammate, they may lose points.

- **Quests** are part of a player's journey that may include various obstacles and challenges that they are required to overcome. You can think of quests like parts of a story. For example, the overall story is about a prince rescuing a trapped princess, but each part of the story such as defeating enemy hordes, surviving the wilderness, and finding the necessary ingredients to make a potion to save her, are all quests.

- **Score** is the total amount of points that the player has accumulated throughout sections of the game. They can be totaled at a specific moment, or at the end of a quest, or even the game. Depending on their importance to the overall objective, will determine how the score is displayed.

Getting elemental

Something to consider when using elements is how will they be obtained by your player? More often than not, when designing gaming experiences, we can be swept up in our own imagination. Adding a badge here and a point there might sound pretty *fun*, but it can become overwhelming to the player, and in some cases they might ask…why? Why am I getting a badge for doing something that I had to do anyway? Because it was fun…right? We will look at using game elements in more detail later in this book, but if you have some ideas now, such as creating an awesome fitness application that will use badges to keep users engaged, ask yourself why you are adding the badge and how it is supposed to keep the player motivated.

In this book, the term game element refers to the Greek word *stoikheion* meaning component or part. Thus, game elements are the *components* of games that contribute to an experience. They include things such as badges, points, levels, and so on. Think about the games that you play. Do they have elements in common? Do most of the games consist of badges, points, and levels?

If you are trying to create a narrative-heavy story, you might consider using elements that are targeted towards immersing the player into the story. For example, quests, narrative, progress bars, and even levels can help to contribute to such an experience. The narrative is what defines the gameplay, quests help to break the narrative into interactive chunks, and progress bars can provide a player with a sense of accomplishment as they advance throughout the game.

If, on the other hand, you want to create a competitive environment, elements such as points, status, levels, leaderboard, and badges can help to facilitate that. For example, a game that encourages students to learn their times tables might compare students against each other in a leaderboard. They are ranked on the amount of questions that they get right: one point for a correct answer minus one for an incorrect one. After a while the points begin to accumulate, the student transcends through different levels; as a result they begin to get a higher status, from Novice Mathematician all the way to Genius. Finally, each level and status is indicated with a badge that is attached to a student's profile.

Before you start to create any game or even add additional elements, look at the games that already exist. Play and play often, because not only will you get ideas about how games use the same elements in various ways, you can get a better idea about whether or not what you are trying to do will work. If you don't have the time to play, watch gameplay videos online (YouTube and Twitch.io). Even walkthrough books can offer a detailed step-by-step guide about how the player is expected to progress through a level.

Getting mechanical

This book refers to the term mechanic based on the late Middle English term (mechanic) meaning *relating to manual labor*. Therefore, *how* a player obtains an element can also be important. Having the *what* is great, but then having the *how* is even better. A player will get a badge, but how they will get it is the mechanic. Does the player have to win, trade, die, or collect certain elements before they can obtain them? For example, does the player have to collect five stars to get the *star badge*? These are considerations that each game designer needs to take into account when adding each new game element. In the following list, we can see a list of common game mechanics, some of which we will be using in the project for this book.

- **Aiming** to direct an object to interact with another or to target an enemy can provide a player with a sense of precision and control, for example, the ability to shoot an enemy that is far in the distance rather than limiting the player to hand-to-hand combat. Aiming can be anything from aiming to kill an enemy or to hit a button from a distance.

- **Building** can allow the user construct parts of the interactive experience. Building can allow the player to develop the environment around them. In games like the Civilization series, building is a core component in gameplay because it can allow the player to advance through the game in various ways.

- **Collecting** allows players to collect items for use later on. Collecting items may be seasonal (such as Christmas) and have expirations (for example, you can only collect items for one week). The main objective here is to let the hoarder free inside of us.

- **Creating** allows users to create their own content. This may be within defined parameters or unrestricted parameters. Creating often allows the user to customize their experience, allowing them to personalize their interaction and adding another layer of personalization. Ultimately, the player has designed something that is *created*.

- **Customizing** allows the user to customize elements of their experience, which can provide a more tailored experience based on what a player likes or doesn't like. Customization may be simple (for example, name change) or extensive (such as name, aesthetics, features, and so on).

- **Disabling** disables features in an interactive experience (for example, location settings and profile privacy), which can provide the player with a sense of authority as well as an option to control the gameplay. This can be disabling buttons to lock out other players, closing doors on enemies, disarming enemies and/or opponents, and so on.

- **Enabling** the player to activate features in an interactive experience (such as location settings and profile privacy). Just like disabling, enabling can be about opening a locked door, and providing enemies with weapons to enable them to progress.
- **Finding** items encourages the user to explore the environment to locate particular items to further the interactive experience. This can be searching chests for a particular weapon, collecting feathers like in Assassin's Creed, or looking for someone in particular to complete a mission.
- **Gifting** another user an item in the form of a gift. This can be to gain rewards for yourself or to provide something for someone else. Who said true altruism is dead?
- **Keeping** items can be as part of an inventory, as collectables, or for use later. Providing the ability for users to keep objects means that they can use them later. Of course, it is possible to limit the amount of objects that a player can keep at any one time, in total or based on the weight. For example, some inventories place emphasis on the amount of *weight* that a player can carry and in some instances items are very heavy, meaning that there is less room for other items.
- **Losing** is not always favorable, but sometimes necessary, especially if we eventually want one victor!
- **Making** allows the user to make items; this is different from creating because a player uses existing elements to make something, for example, providing the user with parts of an item so that they can make it later. It's like finding different parts of a jigsaw puzzle, then ultimately putting them together at the end.
- **Obtaining** items during the interactive experience can be from other players (both real and NPC's), during events (such as from bosses), through performing particular behaviors, and so on.
- **Organizing** items in a particular order (for example, color, shape, size, weight, and so on) can improve a player's efficiency when it's needed such as during an intense battle. Organizing can be manual or automatic depending on what is being organized. Some of the most popular organization options are in inventory systems where players can order the items that they have.
- **Punishing** a player for failing to complete an action correctly can end quite badly for a player depending on how the designer decides to punish them. For example, if they failed to meet an objective within a time limit they might lose the option of getting an achievement, or they might have to begin the entire mission again. It is also possible for other players to deliver and receive, and give to each other. For example, if a player is not contributing enough to a clan or not at a high enough level, it is possible that they will be kicked out and not permitted to rejoin until they reach a desired level.

- **Repairing** items for use at a later stage, even in real-time, can add a range of different experiences. For example, repairing weapons at certain locations within a map encourages players to take more care about how they use them and how often. During real-time situations, such as during an intense fight, players are able to repair their weapons, armor, and so on, in real-time, such as a mech-warrior in Lost Planet 2.

- **Revealing** elements of the experience are revealed or can be revealed if conditions are met. For example, a user will reveal the next level only once they have finished the current one. Revealing can be expected or completely surprising to the player. From a twist in the narrative, location of an enemy, or even the location of an epic weapon, revealing can be as dramatic as you wish.

- **Sending** allows the user to send items, messages, and so on, to other players to increase the social element, which can be a useful mechanic in games where collaboration and cooperation are important.

- **Shooting** another object with a projectile whether it is a grapple hook or bullet to get from *A* to *B* can change the way that a player engages with not only an environment, but also other players (if they are required to shoot them!).

- **Trading** items between individuals or groups can encourage social interaction amongst players. Like sending, trading is also an exchange of items, yet it is reciprocal, meaning that it goes both ways. For example, I will give you this mighty sword for 10 Elderflower potions. If this deal is agreed to, then the trade takes place. Trading systems operate in different ways, such as sometimes you can trade with NPC's within games, or with players. It all depends on how and who you want your players interacting with and what is more important in terms of social interaction.

- **Using** things in games allows the user to engage with a particular feature(s). The ability to use something as opposed to not using it can either create elation or frustration for a player. Imagine you're in the final minutes of the last wave of Zombies, then out of nowhere you see a rocket launcher; unfortunately, it's only there for aesthetics and not for use. This situation can vary the player's overall level of engagement with the game. The world may have been a better place if they could have used it and stopped a Zombie Apocalypse...we'll never know.

- **Voting** allows a player to have a say that can impact future experiences/interactions with the process of voting. Voting may influence the experience of a single user or all users. We can vote to kick a player from a map, to choose a map, to decide on what options are more favorable. Voting brings an element of democracy to your experience, which of course allows players to have a say, but not allowing a system of voting and dictating choices to a player can create an interesting atmosphere.
- **Winning** is what we all strive for when we play games. How a player wins can be anything from natural progression throughout the game, killing a boss, or even choosing to sacrifice your co-op friend for the greater good. I want to lose…said no one ever!

Difference between gameplay and game mechanics

For many, gameplay and game mechanics have subtle differences, if any at all. The main difference, which is presented in this book, is that game mechanics are the basic building blocks of gameplay. Therefore, if we consider the game mechanic list in previous sections, these are *mechanics*, and *gameplay* would then result as a *combination* of these. For example, the combination of *shooting* an enemy to *obtain* items, and *winning* is a gameplay that is typically featured in shooting games.

In any case, while some may refer to the previous list as only *gameplay*, there are other lists that consider them as mechanics, and there are varied definitions about the exact term. The descriptions in this book aim to not only simplify terms, but to also consolidate a list of common vocabulary. Of course, you are encouraged to view other lists and references of game mechanics, some of which can be found at `http://gamestudies.org/0802/articles /sicart`, which provides a comprehensive explanation about the different perceptions, definitions, and approaches to the concept of game mechanics and gameplay; and other lists such as `https://badgeville.com/wiki/Game_Mechanics` or `https://en.wikipedia.org/w iki/Game_mechanics`.

Competency and complacency; where do we draw the line?

Designing games, and more specifically gamified experiences, requires considerations about the type of reinforcement and feedback that the player is given, as well as *how and when*. Too much or too little and they may lose interest. Ideally, it is about balancing the two to keep the player challenged and happy. To begin, let us think about how people are motivated and engaged.

So, you've created a game and you have your first player. At this point, you hope that you will be able to keep them, that they will continue to come back; and if you're lucky, they will share news of their wonderful experience to their friends, and other inhabitants of the Internet. If you extend this to your commercial gamified application, this will be your pass to success. However, for now, let's take a few steps back and think about how we can achieve that.

Let us consider the types of reinforcement and feedback that exist. For example, some focus on the negatives and others on the positives of an experience. Either way has proven successful, but ultimately it comes down to how you want your player to feel. Having a player *avoid* something because it results in a negative outcome, or *avoid* something to optimize the positive outcomes, can lead down different paths in terms of a player's experience.

Examples of feedback and reinforcement

Motivation can be thought of as why we do what we do. Our motivation for engaging with anything is associated with some sort of stimuli that might include a general desire to do so or the need to obtain a reward such as food or money. For instance, let us consider why you are motivated (if at all) to read this book. In some cases, it can determine whether we are short or long-term adopters of anything, from playing a game to buying a new phone.

It does not necessarily imply that we are motivated to do something because we want to; it may be because we are rewarded for doing something and as a result this is our source for motivation. Both are important in understanding how to develop meaningful interactions. For example, if an individual is motivated to learn mathematics by external rewards such as a gold star for doing well on a test, their internal desire is less stimulated with the task and more by the reward. Therefore, how much they *understand* and retain might not be so great as if they were to be genuinely interested.

Understanding how motivation is triggered and stimulated not only provides a necessary grasp of how it occurs, but it also provides insights into how to design in order to trigger and maintain it in a more personal way. Motivation is an important area because it's assumed that identifying triggers and sources of intrinsic motivation will help to identify more meaningful game elements and game mechanics to implement as part of a gamified system. This is with the aim of reducing reliance on extrinsic motivation.

The internal flame for doing...anything

Intrinsic motivation is where an individual's motivation comes from; it's their internal desire to do something for a personal and meaningful reason. If an individual is intrinsically motivated they tend to have a sense of agency in reaching and obtaining their desired goals and as a result are more likely to persist with a task. To understand the different layers that can ultimately affect the level of which intrinsic motivation is likely to occur, we can explore the concept of self-determination theory. It suggests that individuals have three innate needs and that when these three needs are satisfies their intrinsic motivation increases. In the context of games, these three innate needs are:

- **Competency**: How much the game and its associated tasks allow for a sense of accomplishment or mastery?
- **Relatedness**: How much does the game allow for being connected or related with others?
- **Autonomy**: How much the game provide choice over tasks and goals, and sustain the ability to feel a sense of control, as opposed to being controlled by feedback?

If rewards are not used appropriately within the context and value, it can affect their overall motivation to engage with an application or game. If the reward is perceived as praise (such as indicating a level of competency), the reward is likely to increase their intrinsic motivation. On the opposite end of the spectrum, if they perceive that the reward is a form of bribery (for example, to avoid a certain consequence), then it is more likely that an individual will perceive this as compromising their self-determination. The essence of the self-determination theory is built on the notion of meaningful rewards and encouraging intrinsic motivation.

Read this and you'll get candies

In contrast to intrinsic motivation, extrinsic motivation occurs when there are external factors present that influence an individual's behavior. The use of external rewards is what stimulates an individual's extrinsic motivation. If individuals, who are primarily extrinsically motivated, do not receive external rewards for their participation, their interest will eventually decline. Intrinsic motivation individuals appeal more to meaningful feedback, whereas extrinsic motivation individuals are more enticed by the offer of external rewards.

The implementation of external rewards is effective in facilitating extrinsic motivation, but at the expense of intrinsic motivation. To facilitate and promote intrinsic motivation within individuals, there must be less of a focus on extrinsic rewards. While they can be effective at motivating individuals initially, their use cannot be the main trigger of motivations within individuals as this ultimately affects their intrinsic motivation and personal connection to the task, or application that they are interacting with. In this case, the focus needs to be on the intrinsic motivation with the aim of reducing reliance on external rewards that promote extrinsic motivation, in order to encourage intrinsic motivation within individuals. This will not extend the longevity of a gamified application, but it will also reduce negative effects on the individual's self-determination and intrinsic motivation. Unfortunately, there are no candies here, but hopefully you learnt something!

A little bit of conditioning to control user behavior

We cannot understand feedback and reward schedules in games until we have a better grasp on the idea of conditioning. Long ago, psychologists examined how we could develop conditioned responses based on various stimuli. It is important to know these things when our aim is to increase particular behavior or even decrease it.

Classical conditioning

In classical conditioning, a **Conditional Stimulus** (**CS**) is initially a neutral stimulus. Think of something like church bells. However, when it is repeatedly paired with an **Unconditioned Stimulus** (**UCS**), the CS will come to elicit a **Conditioned Response** (**CR**). So, every time that you hear the bells you might remember that it's time to go to lunch at your grandparent's house, and as a result, you begin to salivate because you know you're about to eat. In a standard conditioning procedure, the UCS always follows the CS and the UCS never occurs without the CS.

Repeating the new pairings of the CS and UCS, the CS prohibits the CR from occurring. Thus the CS can be understood to control the CR. Much like our own example, in a well-known experiment, Ivan Pavlov sounded a bell (CS) just before he gave a dog some food (UCS), and after several pairings the bell caused the dog to salivate (CR).

Operant conditioning

The operant conditioning differs from the classical conditioning because it involves applying reinforcement (either positive or negative) or punishment (either positive or negative) after a behavior/response. For example, take the B.F Skinner's infamous rat example, rats really had no reason to pull the lever, except for the fact that when they did, they got some food. Therefore, the rats were *rewarded* for pulling the lever. However, if the food is removed the rats would still continue to pull the lever with the expectation that the food would come again; however if this behavior would become extinct if no food comes out for a long period of time. The other main difference with the operant and classic conditioning is that operant conditioning requires a participant to be actively involved in the process rather than passive. For example, if a child in a classroom behaves appropriately, they will get class points, if they don't, they get punished (for example, detention or time out). Of course this concept is more more deeper than we have time for, but I encourage you to research this topic in more detail on your own, as it relates closely to how players are rewarded when it comes to gamified applications.

Avoid spoiling the player

If we have learnt anything from the previous sections, research (and sometimes common sense) has demonstrated that rewarding the player too much can have side effects such as creating a dependency or reliance on being rewarded. For a moment, let's imagine that you do not want to eat your vegetables. So, as a reward your mother will give you a piece of chocolate if you finish them. This happens continuously until you realize that you want more chocolate. One piece of chocolate is not enough for eating these disgusting vegetables. Therefore, your mother gives you two pieces of chocolate…and so the cycle continues. At what point on this reward merry-go-round do we stop? Until we reach a block of chocolate? Two blocks? It begins to create a dependency, which begins to reduce in satisfaction unless somehow its novelty is renewed with greater rewards. In this way, rewarding a player can be futile in that it provides only a momentary distraction from the issue – like not eating your vegetables.

Let's consider the opposite, such as when you really enjoy eating vegetables. In this case, your mother continues to give you a piece of chocolate every time that you eat them all. This happens again, and again. Ultimately, your mother is rewarding you for something that you already enjoy doing and as a result, you may actually begin to lose interest in it. A big deal was made over something that was unnecessary. This is called *overjustifcation* and can be just as damaging as providing too many rewards.

Finding a balance in providing rewards to a player can be achieved by implementing a reward schedule. A reward schedule can be thought of as an interval timer for when rewards are given to a player. Perhaps early on, the player receives a reward each time they learn a new concept, or achieve something note-worthy. Then, as the player becomes more competent, the time between rewards is increased. By doing this, we are reducing the chances that the player becomes reliant on obtaining rewards.

Summary

Congratulations, you have reached the end! This chapter has offered some insight into the early development of games.

We have covered the basics of; what are games and the types of games that exist? Then we had a brief look at some examples of gaming experiences that are aimed to motivate us when we would rather ignore problems such as a healthier lifestyle, or impending travel plans. Next, we went through brief descriptions of various elements and mechanics that games have and some basic considerations for their use within gaming experiences. Lastly, we looked at understanding motivation and how different types of motivation affect us.

In the next chapter (Chapter 2, *Who or What am I? Understanding the Player*), we will look more closely at players, who they are, where they are from, and what we need to think about when we are designing for them. We will explore the different ways that players can be motivated, and how to facilitate it or to be mindful of it. In addition, we will look at different methods of approaching the design of gamified applications.

2
Who or What Am I? Understanding the Player

There are approximately 7.125 billion humans on planet Earth. Each gaming experience that we design is for a small subset of these people. However, in a world with so many people it can be a daunting task when you need to design a game for any particular audience. With that said, we have a lot in common. We like and dislike similar things, even if they are for different reasons. We have consistent patterns of behavior, which have been observed both in reality (such as personality typologies) and in gaming experiences (for example, player typologies). So that you can get a better understanding about who you will be designing for, this chapter will explore the following topics:

- To begin, *The players – who are they and where are they from?*, will discuss information that relates to who we are, who our audiences are, and how this all relates back to the design of our game.
- Next, *Who our application is targeting*, looks at how to refine our concept so that it becomes more focused around our target audience. What are the aims, objectives, and outcomes? We will discuss important things that we need to consider and how they can influence the overall design of your game.
- This section, *The user*, explains how to implement basic, but foundational user features into our application such as a profile page, an avatar, and some basic player information.
- Before we reach the end of our chapter, *Deciding on what you want your users to achieve* then covers how to set aims and objectives for your players to achieve during the gamified experience.

- Finally, *Creating a user profile system in Unity*, will teach us how to create an achievement page that will come in useful later on in this book. This section will provide an overview, to both the player and to anyone who can view their profile of the achievements that they have obtained and that they are still yet to receive.

By the end of this chapter, you should have a foundation about the different characteristics of players and how they are engaged. This will be useful information when we come to the design part of the project part of this book.

The players – who are they and where do they come from?

Imagine that the next person that you will pass on the street is your future client. It is your job to create a gaming experience that will captivate them; to keep them engaged and curious for long enough to explore the world that you have spent a tireless number of hours perfecting. What do you know about them and what do you *need* to know about them in order to create such a game? A few questions that immediately strike a game designer are:

- Are they someone who responds well to challenges, or do they run from them?
- Do they like games with a good story, or do they prefer action?
- Or is it that they like a combination of the two?

Before we commence with the game designing process, we need to find out more about these things. We do this in order to provide an optimal game environment for not just this person, but for other people like them. For many years, attempts have been made to categorize gamers into what is known as *player types*. Player types attempt to synthesize various traits exhibited during play into player types in order to differentiate an individual's behavior within games. To illustrate this concept, we can refer to Bartle's infamous player types, which were based on the data collected about what users of MUD's experienced as "*fun*", Bartle identified that players fell into one of four categories – Achiever, Socializer, Explorer, or Killer and they are defined as follows:

1. **Achievers** act *ON* the world. They typically play to win in games and feel accomplished through defined goals and progressing with their character through the world's built-in ranking system.
2. **Socializers** interact *WITH* other players and find the greatest reward in games having the opportunity to interact with others.

3. **Explorers** interact *WITH* the world and enjoy discovering new areas and gaining new knowledge of their surroundings.
4. **Killers** act *ON* players and enjoy dominating other players by attacking, killing, or simply making their life hard within the virtual environment.

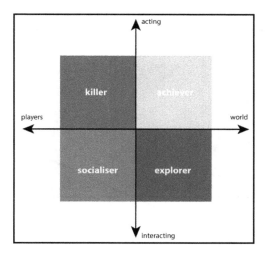

A figure showing Bartle's players.

Not long after the development of the initial four player types, Bartle observed that players tended to fluctuate between the player typologies. In an attempt to cater for these fluctuations, Bartle added another dimension to the traditional model, establishing a further eight player types to his original model:

1. **Opportunists** are *IMPLICIT* Achievers and try to take advantage of a situation any given situation while trying to avoid challenges.
2. **Planners** are *EXPLICIT* Achievers and take the time to plan their actions, with a larger scheme/plan in mind.
3. **Hackers** are *IMPLICIT* Explorers and experiment to reveal meaning and seek to discover new phenomena.
4. **Scientists** are *EXPLICIT* Explorers and experiment within the gaming experience to form theories and explain new phenomena.
5. **Friends** are *IMPLICIT* Socializers and mainly interact with people they already have established relationships with.
6. **Networkers** are *EXPLICIT* Socializers and seek out people to interact with based on assessing and getting to know them.

7. **Grievers** are *IMPLICIT* Killers and are very much in your personal space with the aim of obtaining a menacing reputation.
8. **Politicians** are *EXPLICIT* Killers and manipulate people accordingly to suit their needs as well as acting with well-developed foresight.

The following figure is a representation of Bartle's update to the traditional model:

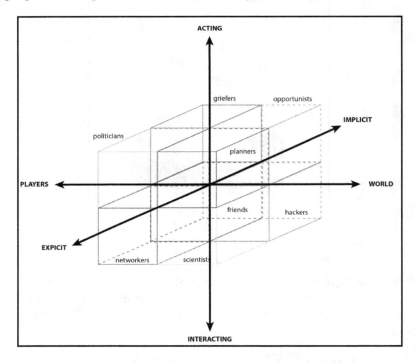

Figure of Bartle's players

Now, at this stage, you might be wondering, what is the point of all this? Why am I reading a book about Gamification in Unity and learning about player typologies? The answer is simple. Not only are these referred to in the development of gamified applications, but they also act as a lens to study the effects of gamified applications (and games in general). It is important to understand that players not only engage with the game or gamified application in a particular way, but also each other. Lastly, while Bartle's typology is perhaps the most well-known typology among player typologies, many others exist; some even criticize the Bartle typology altogether! So, whether you believe in one typology or another, it is definitely worthwhile exploring other types to become more grounded in the concept and to broaden your considerations for players as a whole.

If you want to find out more about Bartle's player types, check out the following book:
Designing Virtual Worlds by *Richard Bartle*.
Other books and publications, which are also recommended:

- *The Proteus Paradox* and *The Daedalus Project* by *Nick Yee*
- *Game Design Workshop: A Playcentric Approach to Creating Innovative Games* by *Tracy Fullerton*
- *Robin's Laws of Good Game Mastering* by *Robin Law*
- *Game On: Energize Your Business with Social Media Games* by *Jon Radoff*

Getting contextual

In the beginning of designing a game or gamified experience, designers need to consider the context for the experience. Context is an important consideration because it can influence the design and development of the game (for example, hardware, resources, and target group). For example, a gamified experience aimed at encouraging students to submit assessments on time and used at school will be designed differently from one promoting customer loyalty and for use within supermarkets. Therefore, a design that is developed through the lens of the context that it is intended for is likely to be more targeted than one designed with a general context in mind. Contexts can be as broad or as specific as the designer wants to get. For now, here is a general list of concepts that you can consider to direct your application towards:

- **Education**: As we discussed in *Chapter 1, The Anatomy of Games*, games can be educational. They may be designed only to teach or they may have elements of learning entwined into them to support learning material. Depending on the type of learning game, it may include formal (educational institutions) or informal educational environments (learning a language for a business trip). Therefore, if you are thinking about creating an educational game, you might need to think about these considerations in more detail.
- Some examples of games that would fit an *educational* context are games that specifically aim to educate or teach concepts ranging from language learning (DuoLingo www.duolingo.com), to understanding physics (Ludwig).

- **Business**: Maybe your intention is get your employees arriving to work on time or finishing reports in the afternoon rather than right before they go home. Designing content for use within a business context targets situations that occur within the workplace. It can include objectives such as increasing employee productivity (individual/group).

  > Games that would fit a *business* context include SimCity `www.simcity.com`, Roller-coaster Tycoon Series `http://www.rollercoastertycoon.com/rollercoaster-tycoon-deluxe`, and Capitalism `www.capitalismlab.com`.

- **Personal**: Getting personal with gamified applications can relate specifically to creating experiences to achieve personal objectives. These may include personal development or productivity, becoming more organized or healthier, and so on. Ultimately, only one person maintains these experiences; however, other social elements such as leaderboards and group challenges can bring others into the personal experience as well.

  > Some examples of games that would fit a *personal* context can be targeted to health and fitness such as Fitbit, various loyalty programs, and lifestyle applications like Fabulous– Motivate Me! `www.thefabulous.co`

- **Game**: If it's not just educational, business, or personal development, chances are you probably want to create a game that provides a portal into lustrous worlds of wonder or to pass the time during a player's daily commute. Pure gaming contexts have no personal objectives (other than to overcome challenges of course!).

  > Games that would fit a *gaming* context and can include anything from Assassin's Creed `www.assassinscreed.ubi.com/en-us/home` to Zork `http://tinyurl.com/ZorkTheGame` and everything in between.

Who is our application targeting?

Due to the nature of gamified experiences relating to players on a more personal level, for example, they target changes in people's daily lifestyles; understanding the user is one of the most important considerations for any approach to be successful. Not only do user considerations include the demographics of the user, for example, who they are, and where they are from, but also the aim of the experience, the objectives that you are aiming to achieve, and outcomes that the objective(s) lead to.

Let's consider a few real-life consequences that your application/game will have on its audience:

- For example, will a loyalty application encourage people to engage with your products/store in the areas that you're targeting it towards? Are you creating a game to teach Spanish to children, teenagers, or adults? This will change the way that you need to think about your audience. For example, children tend to be users who are encouraged to play by their parents; teenagers tend to be a bit more autonomous, but may still be influenced by their parents; and adults are usually completely autonomous. Therefore, this can influence the amount and type of feedback that you give and how often.
- Where is your audience from? For example, are you creating an application for a global reward program or a local one? This will affect whether or not you incorporate things such as localization features, so that the application, adapts to your audience automatically or whether it's embedded into the design.
- What kind of devices does your audience use? Do they live in an area where they have access to a stable Internet connection? Do they need to have a powerful system to run your game or application? Chances are that, if the answer is yes to the latter, then you should probably look at how you optimize your application.

Now that we have some basic ideas outlined about our potential users, it is time to explore who they are in a bit more detail and unpack each of the preceding considerations.

The user

The user is the person or group of people within a particular demographic that you are targeting your experience towards. For example, you could be creating a fitness application for a 22-year-old female business student who lives in Melbourne, Australia. They could be a user who plays games on a regular basis, or someone who has never even played a game, or they could be a combination of the two. As a result, it is important that you define who your user is early on so that each decision that you make along the way is considered through their perspective.

The amount of dedication

Not everyone who plays your game may game on a regular basis. There are varying ends of the spectrum from **Newbie** to **Hardcore** gamers and the following list explains each in a bit more detail:

- **Newbie** gamers are people who are more than likely trying games for the first time. They are from all ages and demographics. When creating games that include these types of gamer, it is important that you have help available. This may be provided in many ways such as walkthroughs from when they first install the game or application to an informative **Help** menu or online support forum.
- **Casual** gamers can refer to people who game less frequently than other gamers do. They may do this on their commute home, to fill in time while waiting at the dentist or at home. They tend to go for games that require a lot of time or commitment, and where the play sessions are short.
- **Core** gamers engage with a variety of different games that usually require a lot more time than games played by a casual gamer. The level of commitment given by core gamers allows them to experience more detailed narratives, complex gameplay, and engage with a more comprehensive experience.
- **Hardcore** gamers engage with every element of the game, from learning, practicing, and memorizing complex button combinations, to studying statics of online virtual currency and trading, managing and running guilds, as well as staying up to date with the latest news on games as well as gaming events.
- **Professional** gamers as the name suggests play to win not just points, but also gain from their skills financially. They tend to participate in competitions at a local, national, and even global level and gain many spectators around the world.

A fun activity to do in order to design for your target audience is to develop personas. These can be fictitious future users that will have a range of different demographics, personalities, and requirements. That way, you can begin to consider different needs of different users.

Defining the role of your player

What your player will do in the game is important, and defining this earlier on can help them to understand not just the purpose of the gaming experience, but also what they need to do to achieve it. In this way, making it clear what the player has to do, as well as shouldn't or can't do, makes it easier for the player to understand their role within the experience.

When we begin to design a game, we may be enticed by our own experiences to have something graphically sophisticated with increasingly difficult challenges and an epic three-headed beast at the end, which we will spend countless hours, blood, sweat, and tears trying to destroy. Then we remember that we are creating a game for primary school kids to learn mathematics. So unless the *mathematic* element is to learn how to count the amount of heads on the beast, then the concept is not ideal. In addition, it is likely that primary school students don't play games for extended periods of time, and are not considered Hardcore gamers. Therefore, a game that requires 48 hours of leveling up, exploring, and battling isn't going to achieve our goals. Therefore, considering the amount of *dedication* that is required from each player earlier on can also give some insight about what the player is required to do.

If you're asking a casual gamer to remember complicated button patterns to finish the first level, either your target group is wrong or you need to modify what you are asking the player to do. Each time that you find yourself wanting to add another element or layer to the gaming experience, ask yourself questions such as: Is adding a three-headed beast going to help teach mathematics or only make the experience more enjoyable?

Deciding on what you want your users to achieve

Consider the following points to determine the end goal for your users:

- **Aim**: The aim of what you want your players to achieve at the end. For example, the aim of your gaming experience may be to increase productivity within users. Ultimately, without a clear aim you can begin to ask what the point of the experience is and why you are designing it. If you are unsure about your aim, chances are the player will be as well.
- **Objectives**: The list of objectives includes different actions that the user must perform to achieve the listed outcomes. These can be anything from finding items, rescuing a princess, and so forth. Some objectives may be hidden and only revealed to the player after certain conditions have been met, such as unlockables. For example, an objective in a language application might be to learn grammar rules and punctuation.
- **Outcomes**: The list of outcomes extends from the aim. For example, for increasing productivity, an outcome involves being more time-efficient. Outcomes may include being able to speak in a new language with a higher level of fluency than when they began.

- **Rules**: Set of guidelines that the user can and cannot do. Rules can be as strict or as open as you want. But make sure that they are clear and that they work. If a player is engaging with your game, you want to make sure that things are black and white. Obviously, any shades of gray are where the player can exploit your system and this can end in all kinds of problems. An important thing to keep in mind once you have begun designing your rules is to play-test them. The same goes for each additional rule that you implement.

Getting the player to achieve it

The type of motivation that a designer wants to facilitate is an important consideration. For example, users can be intrinsically drawn into an experience because they find it interesting without any need for a reward (for example, learning about the history of various civilizations). In contrast, some users may engage with a system purely for the external benefits that it offers (for example, more discounts when they are shopping). If these external rewards are removed, they will disengage. Therefore, finding the right balance between these two, or better yet identifying the type of motivation and designing for it, can be useful. Consequently, it can optimize the experience for the user as well as increasing the longevity of the application for the designer.

One of the most important questions to ask yourself is if it is necessary to reward them for the action, whatever it may be. Like we discussed in Chapter 1, *The Anatomy of Games*, too many rewards can create a dependency, too little then they might lose interest; too much of something that they already like might just kill their motivation entirely.

Engaging the player

As we already mentioned, motivating the player is important if we want to keep them engaged. Motivation isn't just about points but also about providing things that they like in a way that isn't repetitive, but also enough to keep them coming back for more. Three things to consider are in the following list, as well as how they are, and could be, used in your gaming experience; and ultimately taking account of what the short-term and long-term effects are. All have their pro's and con's, so it's about finding out what suits your game and overall approach.

When it comes to motivation, we can think of two main types of motivation, extrinsic and intrinsic. Both can influence the way that you can design a gamified experience and the effect that it will have on the end user. In the following list, each is described in a bit more detail:

- **Extrinsic**: Here is where you want to think about the amount of focus that you will have on the external elements that will motivate your user. To put it simply, extrinsic motivation is the lollies that you offer to a child to clean their room. In relation to the design of your gamified experience, one of the questions at this stage that you will want to think about is are the rewards and feedback that you are providing to the player based on predominantly extrinsic motivation? For example, if you want to reward your player for achieving an objective, is the objective an important one (maintaining a healthy diet for seven consecutive days) or a general one (opening the application on a regular basis). If it's an important one, it is ideal that you give it some attention, either by providing the user with points or a simple acknowledgement such as *Great Work*. Ultimately, how much attention that you allocate is up to you, but keep in mind the impact of rewards and feedback. Some examples may include giving points each time a particular action(s) is performed, but keep in mind that if a player becomes too reliant on points, then it can become an issue in the long term.

- **Intrinsic**: The reason that a user is engaging with your application is more than likely because they want to. Therefore, they are intrinsically motivated. At this stage this is fantastic, you have them there, now let's keep it that way! Some examples could be relating rewards back to their success in a meaningful way. For example, if your application can see that they make more attempts to complete something, the feedback provided once they have finished the task should be encouraging: *Sticking through the hard times has paid off! Bonus 50 points!*

- **Schedules**: The intervals at which events/rewards, and so on, occur are known as schedules. For example, if a user receives a badge once a week for continuing their interaction, then the badge becomes a weekly occurrence. There are two ways that you can offer rewards, scheduled intervals and ratios:
  - Intervals
  - Ratios

Intervals are further categorized into fixed and variable interval reward schedules:

- **Fixed**: Interval reward schedules provide a reward after a certain amount of time has elapsed. For example, after 10 seconds, the player is given a bonus. This can work when you're trying to engage the player for a short period of time; after a longer period of time using fixed intervals, the player's engagement will tend to decrease.

- **Variable**: Interval reward schedules provide a reward after a relatively consistent amount of time. Because this isn't completely consistent, it can keep the player engaged for longer because it is unclear exactly when a reward will be provided. This can provide tension depending on what will be provided after the time has elapsed. The player can estimate the likelihood, but it also decreases the chances for the novelty of rewards to wear off. For example, after roughly one hour a new boss enemy will appear with bountiful rewards for the player to receive once it has been defeated. In such cases, the first in best dressed can be a great way to encourage competition if rewards are single instance per interval.

Just like intervals, Ratio is also categorized into fixed and variable ratio reward schedules:

- **Fixed**: Ratio reward schedules provide rewards after a fixed number of actions have been performed. This is particularly useful when you want players to work towards achieving things such as levels and even status. For example, if you complete 10 tasks consecutively during the week, then you get points towards your progress, if the player fails to achieve this, then they are not rewarded.
- **Variable**: Ratio reward schedules provide rewards after a roughly consistent number of unknown actions has been performed. The benefit of using variable ratio schedules is that the player doesn't know exactly what will happen next, maintaining an element of mystery. This can encourage the player to engage more with the game or application. An example may be if players are exploring lands within a game; exploring ones that are a considerable distance from the mainland (thus requiring more time from the player) is rewarded with a badge.

Getting loopy about engagement

Think about the cycle that a user goes through as they experience your application. Where does it begin and what happens along the way until it begins again? What is the player's journey through your designed gamified experience? Is it infinite like a daily fitness application or is there a definite end such as learning a mathematics topic? In any case, whether infinite or not, there are two types of loop: engagement and progression loops, which players will experience during the gamified experience. These are discussed in the following section.

Engagement loops

They target the micro level of an experience such as the user's actions. These types of loop are used to provide a user with the motivation to perform various actions that are required:

- **Motivation**: Like we discussed before, motivation is what initially brings the user to play your game or application and keeps them engaged *or not*.
- **Action**: This is what we get the player *to do* during the experience in order for them to progress.
- **Feedback**: Providing feedback is extremely important because it indicates to the player how they are going. It can also help them in terms of their level of motivation and their type.

The idea with engagement loops is that each stage feeds back into the next like a cycle, as in the following figure:

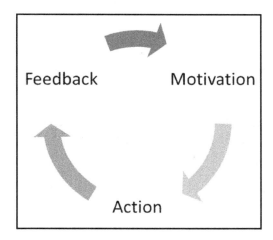

Engagement loop

To summarize, once a user has performed the action, they are provided with feedback. Feedback can be given in a number of ways from points to badges. Once a user receives these rewards, they can often act as a trigger for boosting the user's motivation. An example of this is when a player completes a task such as staying hydrated, where they get points, and they can then buy or upgrade parts of the game, and then begin the cycle again. At a smaller level, progression loops break this process down into chunks.

Progression loops

We can think of progression loops as the overall experience, which may be quite overwhelming in the beginning, and break it down into chunks, or smaller challenges, where each chunk is a step that moves a user from the beginning to the end. Primarily, the first challenge for any new player is to learn the rules and how the game works, and ultimately to find their purpose amongst it all. Then, as they progress, they are provided with challenges that vary and increase with difficulty. This also provides the player with a greater sense of accomplishment and greater satisfaction when they reflect on how far they have come. A basic progressive loop can be seen in the following figure:

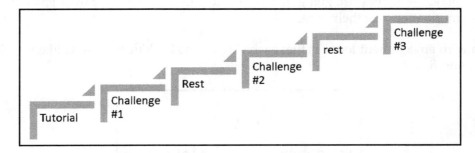

Progression loop

Any journey begins with a single step, and in a gamified system this step can begin with a user. Each user will have a profile, which can be general or detailed depending on the intention of the system and how a profile relates to it. Profiles allow users to carve their identify within the gamified landscape. They are sometimes fictional, alter-egos, other times they are true representations of ourselves. As we are about to learn, setting up a profile system in Unity is a feature that any gamified experience can include to make the experience more personalized for its users.

Creating a user profile system in Unity

Our profile system will include an avatar (a picture of the player), a profile that will include basic information about their location, as well as having their achievements and game elements displayed on a separate page. However, before we embark on creating a user profile system, we need to do a few things, if you haven't already: getting Unity set up and ready to go. Unity exists in different versions: Personal, Plus, Pro and Enterprise. For the purposes of this book, we will be using the free version (Personal), which you can download here: https://store.unity.com/.

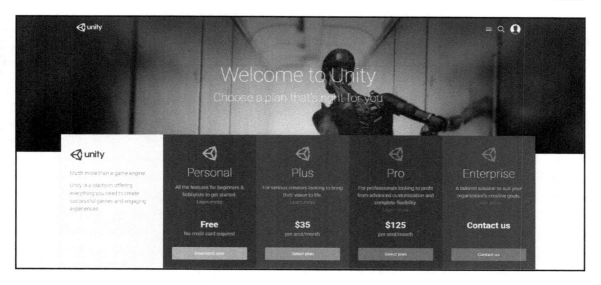

Downloading Unity screen

Setting up the Unity project

Let's begin by setting up a project in Unity. This might sound simple enough, but at this point, *how* you set up your file and folder structure can determine how many headaches you will have later. Another thing to keep in mind during the design and development process is naming conventions, especially for version control. Of course, you are free to follow whatever file structure you like, but make sure it remains consistent. This will save you a lot of trouble later.

To begin, create a new project in Unity by clicking on the **Create project** button.

Then insert the title of your project along with the destination path. Furthermore, since this will be a 2D Application, select 2D, like in the following screenshot:

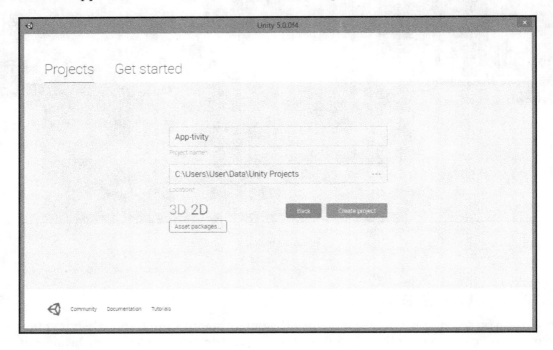

Getting started with Unity

Next, we need to define the resolution of our project. This really depends on what your target platform is. You can change the resolution in the **Game** view like in the following screenshot:

Picture of resolution and aspect ratio

Now we need to import the files that we will be using for this project. These files can be downloaded here: `http://player26.com/`. We can import these files by dragging and dropping them from **Explorer** to the folder that we want them to occupy in the project with a new scene; let's start to create a new image. The image that we need to create will be relevant to the device that you are aiming for, so before you begin it is worthwhile checking the dimensions and resolutions accordingly. A canvas will be created automatically along with the **Event System**. Call it `Background`, and expand it so that it fills the entire screen, like in the following screenshot:

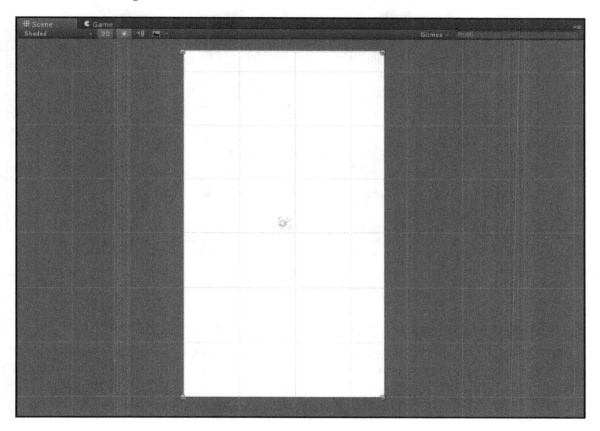

The background

Now, in the **Inspector,** change the image into *[Name of your file]* so we can have a background for our application. We should have something that looks like this:

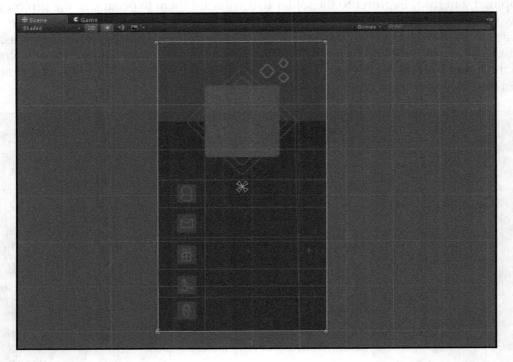

New background

Getting personal with some profile information

Now that we are all set up and ready to go, let's begin with setting up the structure of the profile page. A picture can say a thousand words, but interpretation isn't always a good thing. Having some basic profile information can give your player more of an identity. It can provide them with a bit more than just a name and a face, but some personality. The profile page in this section will have a few elements:

- The profile picture.
- Profile information (name, e-mail, birthday, gender, and location).

Some other examples of information that you can include:

- Clans, guilds, and groups that the player is affiliated with
- Their status and rank within the game or application
- The amount of points that they have in total (this may be trophies, stars, and so on)

Take a moment to look at the following screenshot; this is an idea of what we will have accomplished by the end of this chapter. Take time to look at each element of the profile. You can also think of some other types of information that you think is useful for your application and substitute it or add it to the following design:

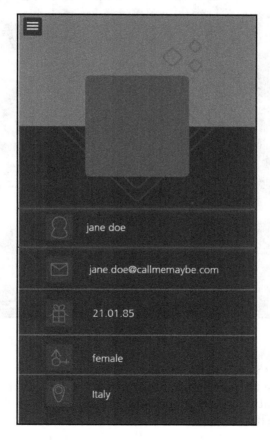

Completed interface

The next step is to insert all of the input fields so that the user will be able to insert their data. Let's create a new field (right-click on the **Hierarchy** panel and then **UI | Input Field**). Then, place it next to the name icon. We need to change the **Transition** to **None (Material)**, and the **Color** of the **Image (Script)** to zero alpha. In addition, change the color of the text to white. Once you have done all of this, you should have something that looks like the following:

Picture of the Inspector

One thing to keep in mind during the development of any application or game is the Canvas hierarchy. One way to think of this is as layers, where the layers at the back will be behind those that are subsequently towards the front. This is important because, if there are some elements that need to be visible, they should be at the top of the hierarchy, so that they are above all of the other layers. If there are backgrounds, they will usually be featured behind all the other layers, therefore, at the bottom of the hierarchy.

Now, one last thing that we need to do is to change the text of the **Placeholder** if you want. For now, we can just use . . . . Of course, feel free to use whatever placeholder text you usually use, and for larger amounts Lorem Ipsum, `www.lipsum.com` is always a simple alternative.

Once we have added the placeholder text, we should have something that looks like the following screenshot:

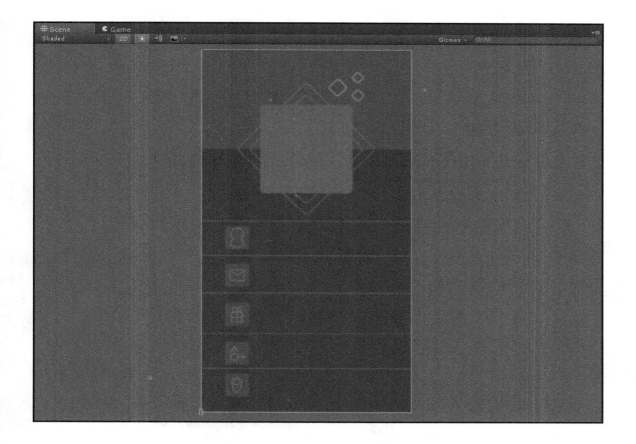

Screen work in progress

We can copy and paste it twice, so that we can cover name, e-mail, and birthday date. We need to change their names and place them correctly in the scene view, next to each of their icons.

If you want, you can use the options of the input field to give some constraints. For instance, you can set the `Content type` of the e-mail input field to be an `email`.

For the gender and the country sections, we need to use the `DropDown` UI component. Let's create it by right-clicking on the **Hierarchy** panel and then **UI | DropDown**. As for the input field, we need to set the **Transition** to **None** and the alpha of the color of the image component to zero. Also, change the text **Color** to white. Then in the **Options** tab, we can change them to suit our needs. To add a new one, press the **+** at the bottom of the **Options** tab; to remove one, select it and click the **–,** in this case, **Male** and **Female**. Now we should have something that looks like this:

The Inspector

After we have placed it next to the gender icon, duplicate it, move it down to the country icon, and change its *Y*-position. Depending on the number of icons your profile page will contain will depend on its value on the *Y*-axis (or even *X*-axis if you're changing the layout!) Therefore, feel free to move any of the icons to locations that better suit your design. Next, change **Male** and **Female** into countries like **Italy**, and so on. Once you have done that, we should have something that looks like this:

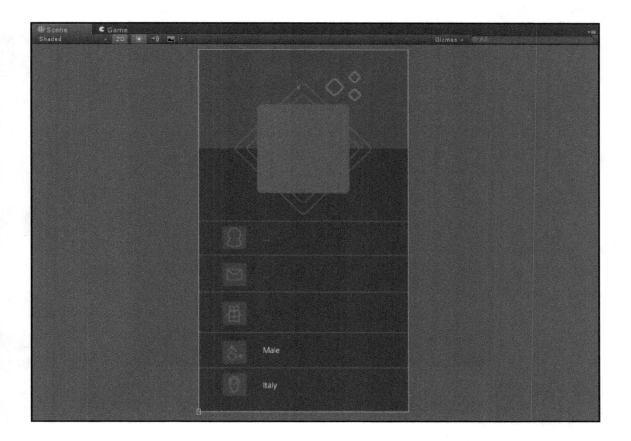

Screen pre-edit button

Showing off that beautiful smile

What is a profile page without a beautiful mugshot? Obviously, it doesn't have to be a picture of the user themselves, but giving users an option to have a profile image is always good. For simplicity's sake, we are providing the user with a predefined selection of images to choose from to put into the profile page like in the following screenshot. Feel free to choose any images that you want and remember, they don't have to be images of people; objects, landscapes, and even cartoon characters are all perfectly acceptable avatars, *dependent on context of course!*

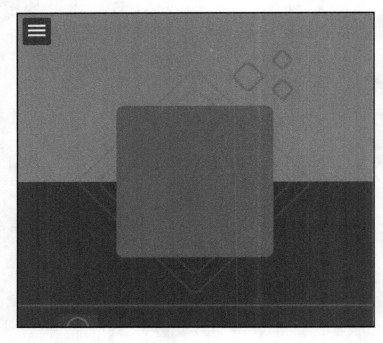

Profile page

Next, we need to allow the user to loop around a series of pictures for their profile, so let's first create a new script. In the **Project** panel in the folder where we want the script, right-click on **New/C# Script**. Name it `ChangeProfilePicture`.

Now, first we need to add at the beginning of the code the following using statement in order to use the UI components in this script: `UnityEngine.UI;`.

Then we need to set some variables. The first is an array of Sprite, where we will set all our images. It has to be public, so we can have access from the **Inspector**. Then we need a counter, that can be private and is an integer. Finally, we need another private variable to get the reference to the UI Image component of the button where this script will be:

```
public Sprite[] profilePictures;

private Image uiImage;

private int counter;
```

Then in the Start() function we need to get this reference to the UI image, so use the following code:

```
void Start () {
    uiImage = GetComponent<Image>();
    uiImage.sprite = profilePictures[0];
}
```

Then we need to create a function to access the counter from other scripts; this will be needed when we need to store this data. So use the following code:

```
public int getProfileImage() {
    return counter;
}
```

Finally, we need a function that will be called every time the user presses the profile picture. In this function, we loop over the picture by increasing the counter, check if it has reached the maximum number of image pictures set, and then assign the new profile picture to the image. So use the following code:

```
public void onClick() {
    counter++;
    if(counter >= profilePictures.Length) {
        counter = 0;
    }

    uiImage.sprite = profilePictures[counter];
}
```

Save the script and now it's time to create a new button. Right-click the **Hierarchy** panel and **UI | Button**. As for the other components, let's set transition to None, and the alpha of the color of the image component to zero. Since here we don't need the text, let's erase it, and leave only the button. Now, let's scale it and place it in the profile picture space. Let's also change the image into the first profile picture we want to have, and this should be the result:

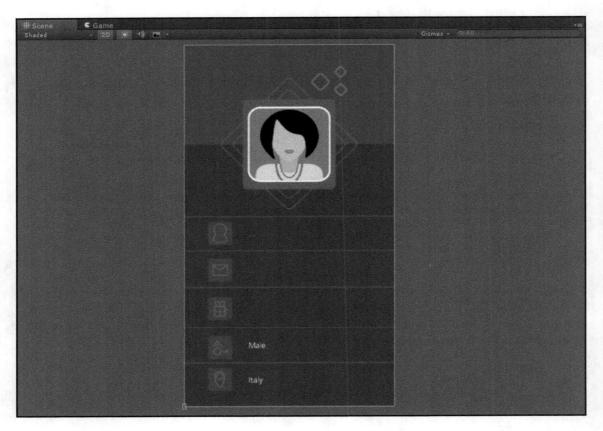

The profile image

Now we need to attach as a component our script that we have just created. Then, we can select our array, change its size, and assign our profile pictures for each of the entries, and it should look like the following screenshot:

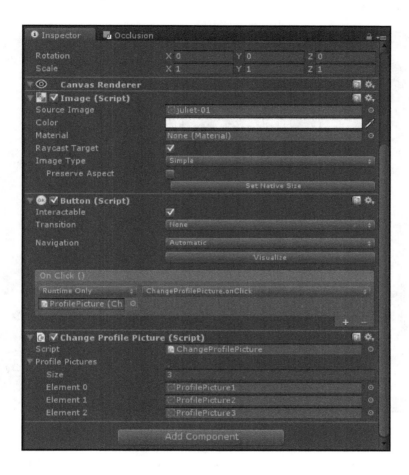

The Inspector

Since we don't want the user to edit their profile all the time, let's create another button. Again, set the **Transition** to **None** and the alpha color of the image component to zero. Finally, change the text into light/gray; as text we can type edit. Now place it as shown in the following screenshot:

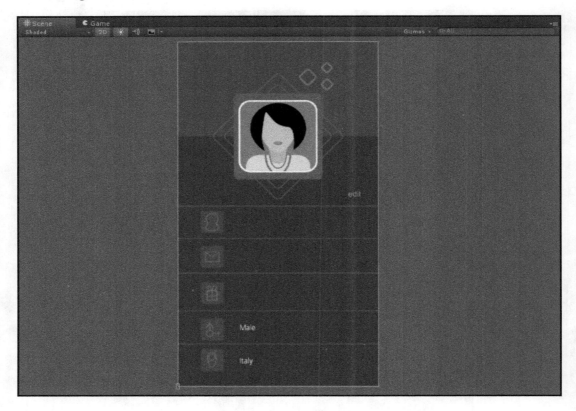

Avatar screen post edit button

Next, in the click tab, let's add some events. In particular, we need to add eight events. Use the first six to get the reference respectively to the name input field, e-mail, birthday, profile, and going in their respective components and set their **interactable** variables to true. Now duplicate this button and call this the done button, and change the text into done. In this new button, disable all the **interactable** variables. About the last two events, on the **edit** button we need to set **SetActive** of the **edit** button to false and in the other event the done button its **SetActive** to true. As in the following screenshot:

Picture of On Click ()

The **done** button will have the same as properties, but in reverse. We need to activate the **edit** button and disable the **done** button, as in the following screenshot:

Picture of On Click ()

Finally, let's disable the **done** button in the **Inspector**, as shown in the following screenshot:

The Inspector

 In general, when enabling or disabling items in the Inspector, make sure that the box next to the item is checked if you want it to be enabled, unchecked, or disabled.

Then, let's set all the **interactable** variables of all the components that we have created to `false` (so uncheck them). If you press play, you can click on **edit** to edit all the data, and once you have clicked **done** you won't able to change them anymore, unless if you press **edit** again.

Summary

As we can see, this chapter covered the basics of creating a player profile system in Unity. To briefly summarize the content covered, we:

- Learnt about user considerations such as how understandings of people began, and how players are defined in games
- Discussed different ways to engage the player based on progression loops and reward schedules
- Explored different ways to set up the player information in Unity in order to provide options to the player for basic customization (for example, change the profile image) as well as options for them to edit their information

Other features that you might consider adding to your player's profile page is information related to their current mood, allowing them to set a status, or even social network handles. You can always check out the official Unity documentation that can be found here: `http ://docs.unity3d.com/Manual/index.html`. Whatever you choose to include, make sure that you consider why you are adding it and whether or not your target group will benefit from it or not.

In the following chapter (Chapter 3, *An Engaged Player is a Happy Player*), we will look at how to engage the player. We will learn about different types of elements, how they can be used to maintain the player's engagement, and keep them motivated to progress throughout the rest of the game. We will also learn how to implement various types of elements in Unity, incorporate a survey, and how to add a social element (for example, social networking services) to your application.

3

An Engaged Player is a Happy Player

Life is better when it's interesting than when it is dull and mundane. It is likely that you have a nice memory of a time when you were playing a game and felt completely immersed and enjoyed the experience; it is also equally likely that you recall when this was not the case. Ideally, as designers, we want anyone that plays our games or uses our gamified applications to have pleasant memories and experiences, and even better to bring others into our worlds of fantasy and enjoyment. Therefore, in this chapter, we will look at the following topics so that we can create an enjoyable experience for your users:

- To begin, *Keeping 'em engaged* will look at ways to provide feedback, reinforcement, as well as track the progress of the player during their engagement with the application. In addition, it will describe ways to engage players throughout the experience.
- Next, *How am I doing?* discusses how gaming experiences report feedback. Whether you provide a player with a brightly colored pop-up saying *FANTASTIC* or have an audio file playing that gives them a verbal pat on the back, we will look at different types of feedback and how to implement them in Unity.
- As we dive further into this chapter, *You've come this far, keep going* looks at the importance of progress for players who want to see how far they have come since they began and reflect on their progress, followed by *Showing off how awesome you are*, which will acknowledge your progress.
- Finally, we finish this chapter with *Taking in the view with Dashboards*. This section shows the player everything at a glance. It looks at the different types of layout that are available and how they display the player's information

- To help improve the design process, *There is no I in Team* talks about agile gamification attempts to change the way that we work not just by ourselves, but also in teams. Therefore, we will look at understanding the different dynamics that this involves when it comes to gamification.

Keeping 'em engaged

Take a moment to think about your gaming experiences. What is it about them that you like? Are you a fan of progression, or do you like to be acknowledged for your efforts? In this section, we will focus on providing feedback to players, and how to keep them motivated and engaged. We will look at different examples of player feedback, such as progress bars, and how can we implement them into Unity.

Feedback can be both positive and negative, and can be provided to the user in more than one way. You can provide encouragement for eliminating multiple enemies with onscreen popups saying things such as *Fantastic* or *Multi-kill!* You can also achieve this by having positive sounds, usually sounds that are pleasant to the ear (such as a chime). In contrast, when a player does something wrong, you can display onscreen messages such as *Fail* or *Incorrect* and, just like positive sounds, you can have negative ones such as a loud horn and so forth. However, just like someone nagging you to put your dirty clothes in the laundry, you don't want to be constantly providing feedback on *everything*, nor do you want to point out every failure. Instead, you want to try to and achieve an even balance of the two and for the right things.

How am I doing?

There are many ways that we can provide feedback to a player. Just like being in school, if you did a test, you were given feedback such as a mark or a *Fantastic* written next to your result. In other cases, if you did something wrong, you will have probably heard your name being called out by the teacher. In this example, you will learn how to create two types of feedback: visual and audio. In addition, feedback can be given in real-time or can be given at the end of an event. When, where, and how the player gets their feedback, depends on what you as a designer are trying (to get the player) to achieve.

Keeping it visual

To create visual feedback within Unity, we need to display a screen to the player. It can contain both a congratulations screen or a retry one. Whatever your feedback is, the way to implement it within Unity is always the same.

Let's start by creating a new image in Unity. Right-click on the **Hierarchy** panel and then **UI** | **Image**. We can rename it `Visual Feedback Screen`. As a **Sprite**, we can use `feedback_pos_screen` or `feedback_neg_screen`. Also, we can use the **Set Native Size** button, giving its original dimensions before scaling it down. If we have created a positive screen, we should have something like the following screenshot:

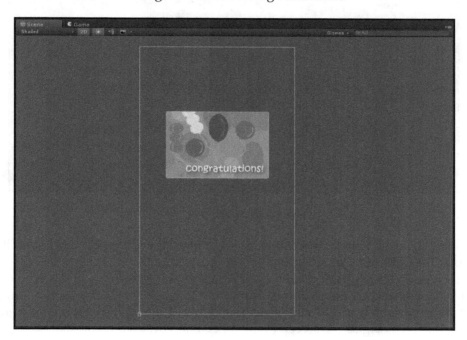

A positive feedback screen

And if we chose to have a negative one, it should look something like the following screenshot:

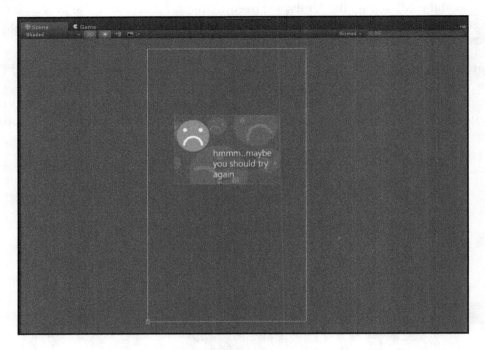

A negative feedback window

Now, we need to add a button that will let the user close the screen by tapping on it. During the creation of the button, we can parent it to `Visual Feedback Screen` if we right-click on it and then go to **UI | Button**. Similarly to what we did for buttons in the previous chapter, we need to set the **Transition** to **None**, and to erase the text by leaving only the button. Furthermore, we need to set the alpha channel of the image component to zero and to make the button as big as the screen (or any size that you prefer, and that suits your design!)

In its **OnClick()** tab, we need to add an event. Drag the `Visual Feedback Screen` into the `Object` variable. Then, select **GameObject.SetActive** and uncheck the box, like in the following screenshot:

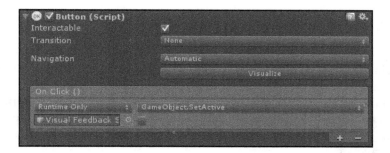

The Button component after we have added the event

As a result, clicking on the button will make the screen disappear.

The next step is to make it appear when an event is triggered. So, in the script where we want to trigger the screen, we need to add a public variable that shows where to get the reference to the Visual Feedback Screen, like this:

```
public GameObject feedbackScreen;
```

Then, when we want to trigger it, we can add the following line:

```
feedbackScreen.SetActive(true);
```

As a result, you are now able to trigger a visual feedback screen in your code.

What's that noise?

Humans have five senses (some may even have a sixth!), so why not tap into one: audio! Audio feedback is even easier to implement within Unity. Instead of creating an entire framework to play sounds, which could make sense if we need to have much more control over the audio, let's just implement a couple of lines of code. In fact, every time we need to have audio feedback, we can create a variable in the script where we want to have the feedback. It stores the audio clip that will be played, like so:

```
public AudioClip audioFeedback;
```

Then, when we need to trigger the audio feedback, add this line of code:

```
AudioSource.PlayClipAtPoint(audioFeedback, Input.mousePosition);
```

As a result, we will have audio feedback. Of course, don't forget to set the variable with the clip in the **Inspector**.

Someone call a doctor!

When you're fighting against an enemy, it is imperative that you know how much life you have left, especially if you have the ability to heal yourself during a high-intensity shoot-out, or when you're the last man standing defending your team's title! In gamified applications, health can also be a way to provide players with a limited number of opportunities to fail, before having a *cool down* period and resuming the experience or prompting them to start again. In either case, health can be displayed in many different ways. You can have a series of hearts, a green bar, or you might have something such as a percentage next to an icon. For the purpose of this chapter, we will create a health counter like the one in the following screenshot. You will also learn the basic skills that you will need to know in order to transform it into any of the types mentioned previously. All these icons can be found at `www.player26.com`:

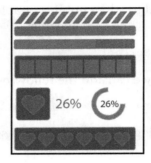

Different health bars in games

Circular health bar

To create a circular health bar, we need a circular picture such as `health_ring`, which you can find in the package:

The health ring that we will learn how to implement in Unity

For this section, let's create a circular health bar as a UI image and rename the game object `Circular Health Bar`. Then, we need to change the **Image Type** to **Filled**.

To properly create the filling of the health bar, we need to set the **Fill Method** to **Radial 360**. As a result, it will be filled in a circular way. Then select **Fill Origin** to **Top**, since we want the health bar to start from the top. Finally, uncheck **Clockwise**, since we want it anti-clockwise. At the end, the component should look like the following:

The Image component after the changes

Next, we need to add a script, as always, in the usual way: **Add Component | New Script**. We can name it `CircularHealthBar`.

Again, we need to use the UI library, so let's add this line at the beginning of the code:

```
using UnityEngine.UI;
```

Then we need a variable to take the reference to the image component, and two additional variables for the actual health value and its maximum:

```
private Image healthbarFilling;
public int maxHealth = 100;
private int health;
```

In the `Start()` function, we need to get the reference to the image component, and set the health to its maximum:

```
void Start() {
    healthbarFilling = GetComponent<Image>();
    health = maxHealth;
}
```

Now, we also need a custom update function for the graphics. Here, in order to compute the percentage, we can divide the health by its maximum. Then, assign the value to the `fillAmount` variable:

```
private void updateHealth() {
    healthbarFilling.fillAmount = health / maxHealth;
}
```

The next step is to create a function to add health to the user. If it reaches the maximum, the health is capped; otherwise, it will just increase. Finally, the graphic is then updated by calling the function we created before:

```
public void addHealth(int value) {
    health += value;
    if (health > maxHealth)
        health = maxHealth;
    updateHealth();
}
```

The trivial part is a function that subtracts health from the user, because it may reach zero. So, we need to have a Boolean to return a value that indicates if this event happens. In fact, when we call this function, through the return value we can understand if the user has finished his or her health and perform a consequent action. Therefore, we need subtract the value from the health, and then we check if the total health is zero. Before returning the value, we update the graphic as well:

```
//Returns true if the user dies
public bool removeHealth(int value) {
    health -= value;
    if (health <= 0) {
        health = 0;
        updateHealth();
        return true;
    }
    updateHealth();
    return false;
}
```

Save the script, and we have implemented a circular health bar!

Lives counter

While we are playing, and especially if we are encountering enemies that affect us, we need a lives counter to keep track of how long we are able to survive within the game and whether or not we need to get med packs. Just like the health ring, we can also display lives with a counter graphic, such as in the following screenshot:

Health bar counter with hearts

We are going to create this type of counter, but you are welcome to use another image instead of hearts.

To begin, we need to have a background box where to place our hearts. The `health_background` file in our package will serve to the scope. So, let's create a new image, set it as a Sprite, and name it **Lives Counter**. Furthermore, remember to use **Set Native Size** before scaling if you want to keep the proportions. At the end, we should have something like the following:

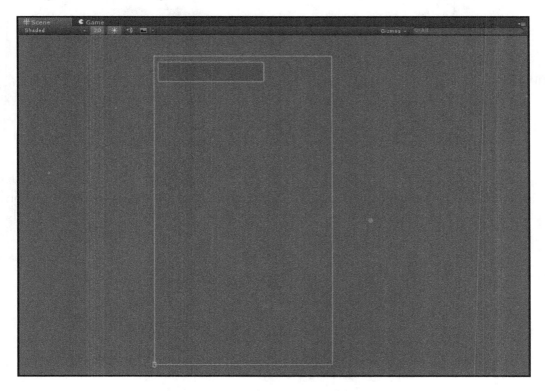

Creating the heart bar

Then, we need to have a heart; in this case we can use the heart from the package mentioned earlier. We need to create five images with the heart as a Sprite, and then place them like in the following screenshot:

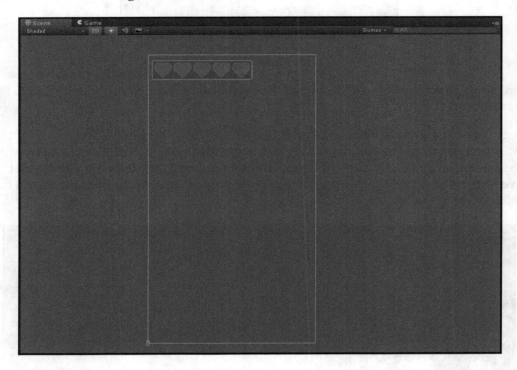

The completed graphics of the heart bar

It's important to name them in the correct order to avoid headaches later on. The heart on the left will be `Heart_01` and they'll be numbered consecutively towards the right, until `Heart_05`. In addition, we need to parent them to **Lives Counter**, as shown in the following screenshot:

The game object parenting of the Lives Counter in the Hierarchy panel

Now, let's add a script to **Lives Counter** and name it `LivesCounterScript`.

First, we need to add a couple of variables, one to store the reference to all the hearts (an array will be fine) and another one for the actual number of lives:

```
public GameObject[] hearts;
private int lives;
```

Then, in the `Start()` function, we need to assign the number of lives according to the number of hearts we have:

```
void Start() {
    lives = hearts.Length;
}
```

As usual, we need a custom `update` function. We need to disable only the hearts that have a number, or index, greater than the actual number of lives. A `for` cycle will work:

```
private void updateLivesCounter() {
    for (int i = 0; i < hearts.Length; i++) {
        if (i < lives) {
            hearts[i].SetActive(true);
        }
        else {
            hearts[i].SetActive(false);
        }
    }
}
```

In the function to add a life, we only need to check if the user already has the maximum number of lives, and then update the graphics with the function we wrote before:

```
public void addLife() {
    if (lives < hearts.Length) {
        lives++;
        updateLivesCounter();
    }
}
```

As we have done before with the health bar, we also need a function to remove a life and check if the user has lost all of his or her lives. Therefore, we again need a Boolean return value: if its is `true`, then the user has finished their lives. As a result, when you call this function from your scripts, you will be able to perform an action accordingly. So, let's write the following:

```
public bool loseLife() {
    lives--;
    if (lives > 0) {
        updateLivesCounter();
        return false;
    }
}
```

Save the script, but we aren't done yet. In fact, in the **Inspector**, we need to assign our hearts like in the following screenshot:

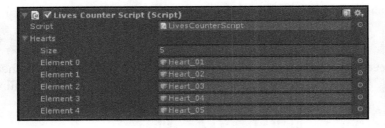

The Lives Counter with the array of Hearts filled

Now, we have finished, and your **Lives Counter** is ready.

On point!

Points can come in various ways. A player can obtain points by defeating an enemy, doing the right thing, or even working cooperatively with other players. Now we have worked on a lot of images, this section shows us how to use the text component to implement a **Point System**.

Let's start by creating a text component. To do this, right-click on the **Hierarchy** panel and then select **UI | Text**. We can rename it `Point System`. Feel free to customize it as you want by changing the font, size, and so on. It doesn't matter what text you put in it, because it will be replaced by our script, but we can use anything as a placeholder. In this case, we can write `Points: 100`. Once we have done all of this, we should have something that looks the following screenshot, in the **Scene** view:

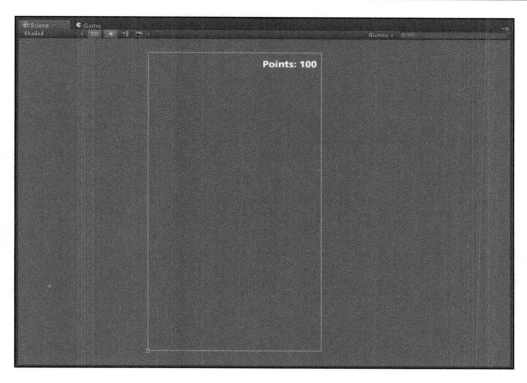

The points system in Unity

Now, let's add a script and name it `PointSystemScript`. Since we are going to use UI components, let's import the library by adding the following line at the beginning of our script:

```
using UnityEngine.UI;
```

We need two variables, one to store the reference to the text component, and the other one to store the actual number of points. Since there might be a lot of points can be a lot, it's better to use `long` instead of `int`:

```
private Text uiText;
private long points = 0;
```

Since the points could be useful on different occasions, such as unlocking achievements, it's better to have a `get function` to retrieve their value:

```
public long getPoints() {
    return points;
}
```

In the `Start()` function, we can get the reference to the text component, and call our custom update that we are going to write in the next step:

```
void Start() {
    uiText = this.GetComponent<Text>();
    updatePointsSystem();
}
```

In the custom update, we need only change the text variable of our text component with the number of points. Don't forget to add a header, such as `Points:` (with the space!). So, let's write the following:

```
private void updatePointsSystem() {
    uiText.text = "Points: " + points;
}
```

Finally, we need a simple function to add points to our counter:

```
public void addPoints(int ammount) {
    points += ammount;
    updatePointsSystem();
}
```

Save the script, and you have implemented the points system. You should have found this step easier to follow, after we have done all the progress and health bars. In the next section, we will see how to make achievements.

You've come this far, keep going

This section will discuss ways to monitor an individual's progress, as well as display it.

We will be populating it with various icons, which can be downloaded from `www.player26.com`, and can be seen in the following screenshot. These icons are available in six different colors (magenta, yellow, blue, green, orange, and red) and three different styles (flat, glossy, and colored). These icons will represent basic things within the game, such as lives, achievements, events, unlockables, and mystery items. However, feel free to add or even change their association to suit the kind of game or app that you are creating:

Different icons to choose from

Making progress

As humans, after we commit a certain amount of time and effort to something, we want to see our progress. Progress bars are excellent ways of demonstrating this. They can be designed in many different ways, for example, they can be segmented, where each segment represents a part of the overall progress towards something. Another way is similar to a health bar; it's a colored meter that fills up over time as the player gains experience. We will learn now how to develop a basic progress bar such as in the following screenshot:

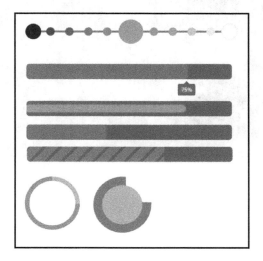

Different types of progress bar implemented in Unity

In order to create our progress bar, we first need to add a new UI image by right-clicking on the **Hierarchy** panel and then selecting **UI | Image**. As a Sprite, we need to assign `progress_bar_blue_background`. To keep its original dimension, let's press the **Set Native Size** button, and then scale it down uniformly (holding the Shift key). Rename it **Progress Bar Background**. As a result, we should have something like the following screenshot in the **Scene** view:

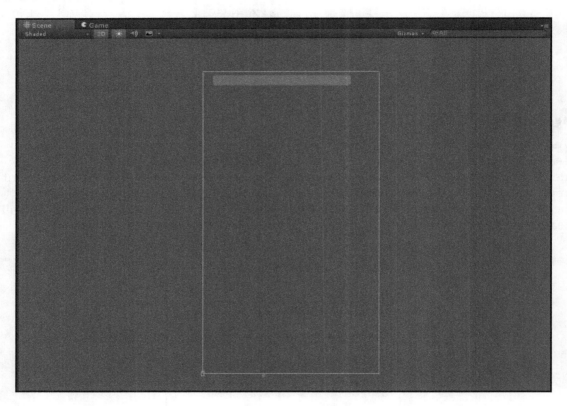

The progress bar background

The next step is to create another image, which will fill our progress bar. Repeat all of the preceding steps, but use `progress_bar_blue_overlay` as the Sprite. Rename this other one `Progress Bar Overlay`. Once you have made the last one, overlay the previous image, and you have the following the **Scene** view:

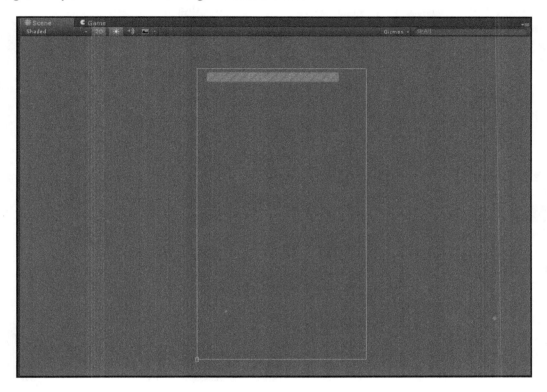

The completed progress bar image

Since we want to show the percentage of the progress bar as well, we need to create a text component by right-clicking on the **Hierarchy** panel and then selecting **UI | Text**. Rename it `Progress Bar Percentage`. Feel free to make it look like you want. In this example, we just changed the text color to white and placed it in the middle of the progress bar. Once you have done all this, you should have something that looks like the following:

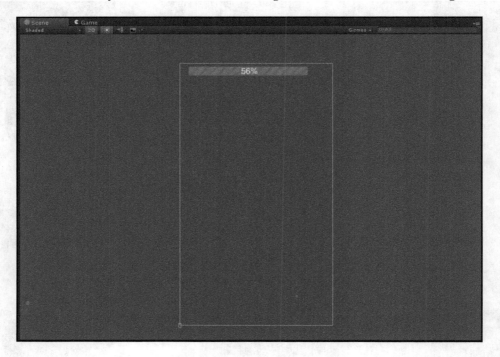

The complete progress bar with the percentage displayed

Now, let's parent the **Progress Bar Overlay** to the **Progress Bar Background**, and **Progress Bar Percentage** to **Progress Bar Overlay**. As a result, our Hierarchy should look like the following:

The game object parenting of the progress bar in the Hierarchy panel

Before we start adding our script, we need to prepare the **Progress Bar Overlay**. In the image settings in the **Inspector**, change the **Image Type** to **Filled** so we can change how much it is *filled*. Since we want a progress bar that goes from the left to right, we need to set **Fill Method** to **Horizontal** and **Fill Origin** to **Left**. This is what the **Inspector** at the end of these changes should look like:

Screenshot of the image component after the changes

Now, we are finally ready to add a script. Let's create a new script by clicking on **Add Component | New Script**; rename it `ProgressBarScript`. Double-click on the script to open it.

The first thing that we need to do is to add the library that allows us to use UI classes. This can be done by adding the following line at the beginning of the script:

```
using UnityEngine.UI;
```

Then, we need to add some variables. A couple of these variables will be needed to keep track of the UI components, and another one for the progress. So, let's write the following:

```
private Image progressbarFilling;
private Text progressbarText;
private int progress = 0;
```

In the `Start()` function, we need to get the references to the UI elements. For the image we can just call the `GetComponent()` function. However, for the text component, we need to get it from the child of the game object. We want our bar empty because we need to update the graphics with a function that we are going to write after this. So we can write the following:

```
void Start() {
    progressbarFilling = GetComponent<Image>();
    progressbarText = GetComponentInChildren<Text>();
    updateProgressBar();
}
```

Then, we need a function that updates the graphic. We don't use the `Update()` function because it is called in every frame. Also, there is no need to update the progress bar in every frame, but only when it changes its value. In particular, we need to update the quantity of filling and the text in percentage form. Since `progress` is a value from *1* to *100*, if we divide it by *100*, we will obtain a fraction from *0* to *1*. In fact, this is required for the `fillAmount` variable. So, let's write the following:

```
private void updateProgressBar() {
    progressbarFilling.fillAmount = progress / 100f;
    progressbarText.text = progress + "%";
}
```

Finally, we need a function that can be called from another script or event to increase the `progress`. Furthermore, if the `progress` reaches 100%, we should add a piece of code to trigger what we want at the end. So, let's write the following:

```
public void increaseProgressOf(int value) {
    progress += value;
    if (progress >= 100) {
        progress = 100;
        //Trigger an action when the progress Bar is complete
    }
    updateProgressBar();
}
```

Save the script.

Now our progress bar is ready to use.

Showing off how awesome you are

What's the point of having achievements without showing them off? Maybe you want to feel like you have accomplished something after a long day of work, or maybe you just want to show off your shiny new badges to your friends. That is why we will be creating a profile page with our achievements included. The basic screen that we will have after this section looks like the following screenshot:

The Achievement page

Badges, badges, badges

Now it is time to implement some badges that are based on the player's achievements. An example of what the finished product will look like can be seen in the following screenshot. For now, we will be using the icons from `www.player26.com`, but feel free to use any other images that you may have:

Completed badge part of the application, featuring (left) the unlocked version and (right) the locked version

Achievement unlocked!

Items that are locked can create a mystery about what they actually contain. Do they have some rare item, lots of gold, or maybe it's something exclusive to a particular thing? As humans, we are curious, and unlockables can drive that curiosity. In some cases, trying to figure out *how* to unlock whatever is hidden can drive us mad:

Examples of other unlockable icons

Implementing an achievement system

The first thing to do is to create a new image component in Unity. As we did for the profile picture in the previous chapter, it must be full-screen. We can use the `achievements_page` in our package. It's always useful to give meaningful names to all the game objects we create. For instance, we can rename it `Achievements Page`. This is the result:

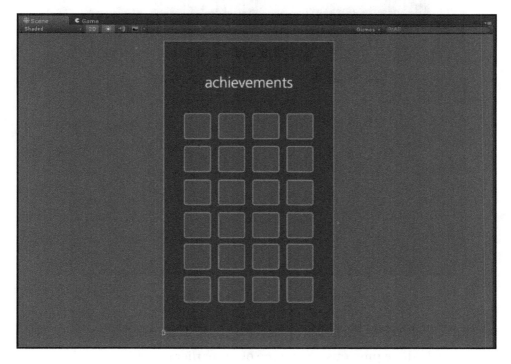

The Achievement Page without any achievements

Now, we need to create another image using `epic_clicker_greyscale` from our package. For the same reasons as before, name it `Achievement_1`. We need to both scale it to fit the first space in the `Achievements Page` and parent it to the `Achievements Page`. So, at the end we will have something like the following:

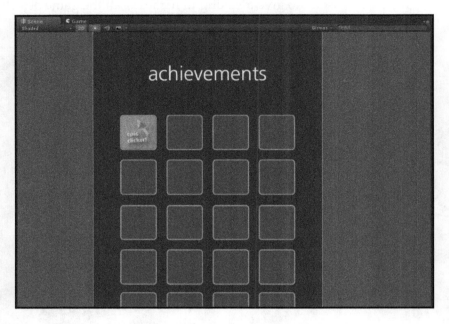

The achievements page with the first achievement (in its locked state)

Create a new script attached to `Achievement_1` and name it `AchievementScript`.

As we have already done previously for some of the earlier scripts, we need to import the library that contains the UI classes. This can be done by adding the following line at the beginning of our script:

```
using UnityEngine.UI;
```

We need to add three variables, two for storing the reference to both the locked and the unlocked sprites, and the third for the reference to the image component. So we can add the following:

```
private Sprite lockedSprite;
public Sprite unlockedSprite;
private Image uiImage;
```

Then, in the `Start()` function, we need to get the reference to the image component and the locked Sprite:

```
void Start () {
        uiImage = GetComponent<Image>();
        lockedSprite = uiImage.sprite;
}
```

Finally, we need to create a couple of functions to unlock and to lock again (if needed, for instance, to reset the achievements). We just assign the new (or old) Sprite to the image component as follows:

```
public void unlockAchievement() {
        uiImage.sprite = unlockedSprite;
    }

    public void lockAchievement() {
        uiImage.sprite = lockedSprite;
    }
```

Now, save the script.

In the **Inspector**, we need to assign the unlocked Sprite. We can drag `epic_clicker_coloured` from our package into the `unlockedSprite` variable, as in the following screenshot:

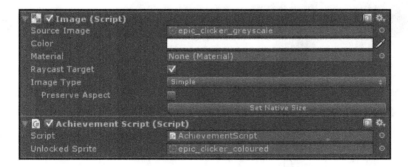

The image component along the achievement script with the variable filled

Next, we can trigger the achievement to unlock it. Once it is unlocked, it will look like the following:

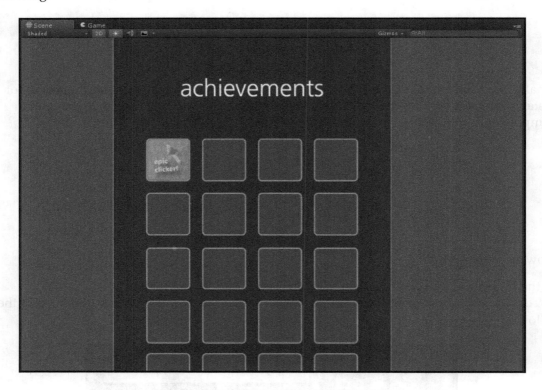

The achievements page with the first achievement (in its unlocked state)

Example of usage

This section will show a simple case of using the script that we have created before.

Let's create a new button. In its **On Click ()** tab, create a new event and bring `Achievement_01` into the `Object` variable. From the drop-down menu, let's choose **AchievementScript | unlockAchievement()**, as shown in the following screenshot:

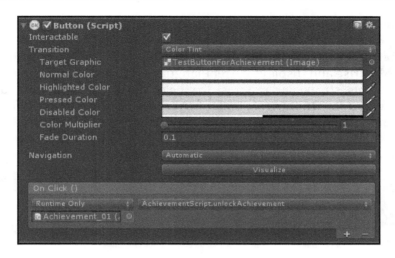

The button component with the event to trigger the unlocking of the achievement

As a result, when the user clicks on the button, the achievement will be unlocked. Of course, this will work much better if we include a visual or an audio feedback, as we have already discussed.

Getting badges, points, and progressing in a gamified experience should all be displayed somewhere. We need a nice place, to display our trophies and to reflect on all that we have accomplished, so far. Dashboards are a great way to achieve this. Not only do they provide summaries of your overall experience, but they are great to way to really feel as though you have accomplished something, and to see where you need to head next, albeit unlocking achievements or progressing to the next level. Just like many things, dashboards can be as complex or as simple as the designer wants to make them, but remember that they need to be meaningful. It should not only be about what you want to show to the player, such as their progress, but also why you want to show it.

Taking in the view with dashboards

Overviews, summaries, and simplicity make life easier. Dashboards are a great way to keep a lot of information relatively concise and contained, without being too overwhelming to a player. Of course, if the player wants to obtain more detailed information, perhaps statistics about their accuracy since they began, they have the ability to do so.

So, what exactly is a *dashboard*? A dashboard is a central hub to view all of your progress, achievements, points, and rewards. If we have a look at the following screenshots, we can get a rough idea of the kind of information that they display. The image on the left is the dashboard for **Memrise** and displays current language courses, in this case German, the player's achievements, streak, and progress that he or she is making in the course. On the right is the dashboard for **DuoLingo**. Similar to Memrise, it also features information about daily streaks, amount of time committed, and the strength of each category learned for the new language, which in this case is Italian. By just looking at these dashboards, the player can get a very quick idea about how well or *badly* they are doing:

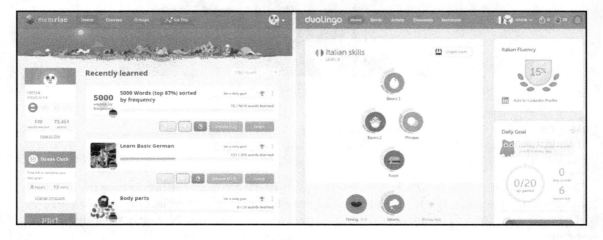

Different dashboards: Memrise (left) and DuoLingo (right)

Different approaches to dashboards can encourage different behaviors depending on what data is displayed and *how* it is displayed. For example, you can have a dashboard that provides reflective information more dominantly, such as progress bars and points. Others can provide a more social approach, displaying the player's rank among friends, and comparing their statistics to others who are also engaging with the application. Some dashboards may even suggest *friends* that have similar elements in common such as the language being learned.

Ideally, the dashboard's design can be as simple or as complicated as the designer decides, but typically, the *less is more* approach is better.

Now so far, we have gotten our feet wet with the world of Unity. From the beginning of this book, we have discussed users, implementing some features of our application in Unity, and some theoretical underpinning of what gamification is all about. We have a profile page, some health, progress bars, and they are all nice enough but, when it comes to developing our application on a larger scale, we need to consider how to work as part of a group. For example, we don't always have access to icons and image packs, nor do we possess all the skills that we need to get our application where we want it. Therefore, we need a team, and more importantly we need to know how to work with others. In order to work in a team, we need a workflow process, some methodologies to ensure that things run smoothly and the project (and its parts) are finished and ready to be implemented within a scheduled timeframe. The following section will look at what it means to work as part of a team and what agile gamification is all about. While working by ourselves, we are able to achieve great things, but when working with others, we can turn them into extraordinary things.

There is no I in team

Working on our own can be good, but *sometimes* working with others can be better! But the problem with working in a team is that we're all not equal. Some of us are driven by the project, with the aim of getting the best possible outcome. Others are driven by fame, reward, money, and the list goes on. If you have ever worked on a *group* project, then you know exactly what it's like. Agile gamification is, to put simply, getting teams working *better* together.

Often, large complex projects encounter a wide range of problems, from keeping on top of schedules, different perspectives, undefined roles, and a lack of overall motivation. Agile frameworks in this context are associated with the term Scrum. This describes an overall framework used to formalize software development projects. The scrum process works like this:

1. The owner of the product creates a *wish list* known as the product backlog.
2. Once the sprint planning begins, members of the team (between 3-9 people) take sections from the top of the product backlog. Sprint planning involves the following:
   1. List all of the items that need to be completed for the project (in story format: who, what, and why). This list needs to be prioritized.
   2. Estimate each task relatively (using the Fibonacci system).
   3. Plan the work sprint (1-2 weeks long, but less than 1 month long), working towards a demo.

4. Make the work visible by using a storyboard: *to do, doing, done*. Items begin in the *to do* section. Once they have begun, they move to the *doing* section, and once they have been completed, they are put in the *done* section. The idea is that the team works through tasks in a burn down chart. Ideally, the amount of *points* that the sprint began with (in terms of tasks to be done) decreases in value each day, the closer you get to finishing the sprint.

 Trello is program that does story boarding like this: www.trello.com.

5. The team engages with daily meetings (preferably standing up) run by the sprint/scrum master. These meetings discuss what has been done; what is planned to be done during the day; any issues that come up, or might come up; and how can improvements be made.

6. Provide a demonstration of the product's basic (working) features. During this stage, feedback is provided by the product owner relating to whether or not they are happy with what has been done, the direction that it is going, and how it will relate to the remaining parts of the project. At this stage, the owner may ask you to improve it, iterate it, and so forth, for the next sprint.

7. Lastly, the idea is to get the team together and to review the development of the project as a whole, what went well and what didn't go so well. What are areas of improvement that can then be used to make the next *scrum* better?

3. Next, they decide on how to implement each section. They will meet each day to not only assess the overall progress made for the development of each section, but to ensure that the work will be achieved within the timeframe.

4. Throughout the process, the team leader known as the scrum/sprint master has the job of ensuring that the team stays focused and completes sections of the product backlog on time.

5. Once the sprint is finished, the work should be at a high enough level to be shipped, sold to the customer, or to at least shown to a stakeholder.

6. At the end of the sprint, the team and scrum/sprint master assess the work completed, and determine if it is at an acceptable level.

7. If the work is approved, the next sprint begins. Just like the first sprint, the team chooses another chunk of the product backlog and begins the process again.

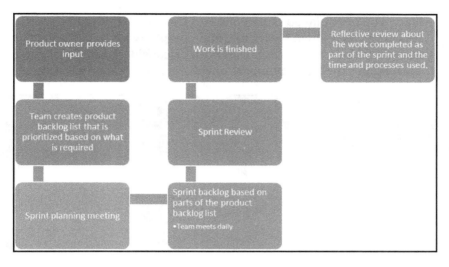

An overview of the scrum process

However, in the modern world, *scrum* has been adopted and applied to a range of different contexts outside software development. As a result, it has gone through some iterations, one of which includes gamification. *Agile gamification*, as it is more commonly known, takes the concept of scrum and turns it into a playful experience.

Adding an element of fun to agile frameworks

To turn the concept of *scrum* into something a bit more interesting and at the same time boosting the overall motivation of your team, certain parts of it can be transformed with game elements. For example, implementing leaderboards based on the amount of tasks that each team member is able to complete (and on time) results in a certain amount of points. By the end of the sprint, the team member with the most points may be able to obtain a reward, such as a bonus in their next pay or an extended lunch break. It is also possible to make the burn-down chart a bit more exciting, such as placing various *bonuses* if certain objectives are met within certain timeframes, or at a certain point during the *burn-down*, giving added incentive to team members to get things delivered on time as a result. In addition, to ensure that quality standards are also maintained, *scrum/sprint masters* can also provide additional rewards if there is little or no feedback regarding things such as quality or the overall cohesiveness of the output from the sprint. An example of a gamified framework can be seen in the following screenshot. While setting up a DuoLingo classroom account, users are presented with various game elements, for example, a progress bar shows how much of the setup the user has completed, and a checklist ensures that everything that needs to be completed is done.

Have you ever played Dungeons and Dragons? It might be worth checking it out when trying to come up with ways to design challenges for a sprint. The scrum/sprint master can be considered like the Dungeon Master, and the team members like those embarking on the quest.

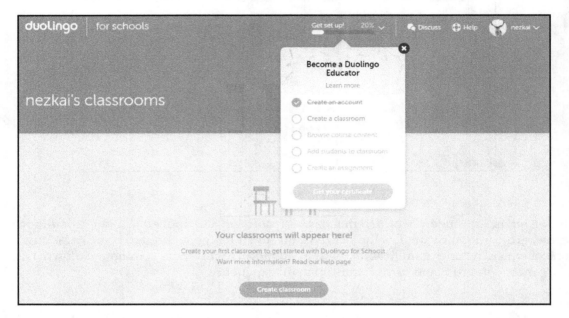

Gamification of the process for setting up a DuoLingo classroom

Here are some useful links and resources if you are interested in learning more about scrum and how the process can be gamified:

- Agile gamification: www.agilegamification.org
- Acle Leagues: www.agileleagues.com
- Lego4Scrum: www.lego4scrum.com
- Scrum Alliance: www.scrumalliance.org
- Scrum: www.scrum.org
- ScrumHub: www.scrumhub.com
- Scrumble: www.scrumble.pyxis-tech.com

Summary

This chapter has covered topics in Unity for keeping the player engaged and looked at different ways to approach this. Next, we looked at how we can encourage the player and indicate their progress with different types of feedback, both in visual and audio ways, to indicate to the player right and wrong actions. Then, we learned how to implement various game elements in Unity, such as health indicators (a circular health bar and a lives counter), progress bars, badges, and points. After this, we looked at gamification dashboards, their design, and their overall objective. Lastly, we discussed what it means to work with agile gamification and keeping a team motivated.

Overall, in this chapter, we have seen how to create different game elements that can be reused (and we will reuse them in the next chapters). We have also used some of the knowledge acquired from the first two chapters to better understand and create these game elements.

In the next chapter (Chapter 4, *Organized Chaos – Getting Ideas Out of Your Head and on to Paper*), we will be looking at creating the application that we'll focus on during the rest of the book. We begin by learning how to effectively brainstorm ideas, get them out of your head into a more organized and coherent idea, refine them, and finally get something happening in Unity.

4
Organized Chaos - Getting Ideas Out of Your Head and on to Paper

At any one moment, we will have ideas entering our minds, even thousands will come and go during a day. So how can we gamify all these ideas? In this chapter, the reader will learn how to design a gamified application before starting to create a final version. The reader will learn different and specific techniques for the creation of gamified applications in different contexts, allowing the reader to have more tools to face the challenge. Furthermore, you'll also learn how to use Unity during the process to help the reader to create helpful tools in Unity to generate new ideas. Here's a list of topics that we'll cover in this chapter:

- To begin, *Brainstorming–getting it all out on the table* discusses the concept of brainstorming and what kind of thing needs to be considered along the way.
- Next, *Tools and methods for getting ideas out and organizing thoughts* will look at various tools and techniques for getting the ideas of your own as well as other members of the team out in the open in a more organized way.
- Then we will learn how to brainstorm in *Brainstorming activities*, where we will see different ways to brainstorm, which will give you a starting point to get the creative juices flowing.
- Finally, *Implementing a brainstorming tool in Unity to shuffle ideas*, is where we take some preliminary ideas and implement them into Unity. Instead, we will learn that Unity will be a *random idea generator* that will randomize ideas if a group is having a hard time to decide on one. It can even be used as a thought/idea generation tool, depending on the kind of input that the reader decides to implement.

Brainstorming – getting it all out on the table

This section will focus on brainstorming for the project that we will be creating in this book.

Ideally, when it comes to brainstorming parts of your game, you want to think about everything, not just the art style. Here are some examples of things to consider:

- **Game concepts** are based on the kind of game that you want to create. What are the types of theme that your game will be influenced by? Do you want to create something like Zombies! Run (www.zombiesrungame.com) that focuses on a player getting fit by having to run away from hordes of zombies?
- **Game-play experience** is what the overall experience will be like that you want your player to engage in. Do you want a fast-paced kind of experience or something that progressively builds up challenges? Take a moment to think about this; even if you have a basic idea, it can help to guide you during the brainstorming process.
- **Game elements and mechanics** as we discussed in Chapter 1, *The Anatomy of Games*, is how the game interacts with the player and vice versa. Each time a player achieves an objective, what happens and *how* does a player achieve an objective in the first place? Again, a basic idea at this stage is all that you need. Ideally, you want to have a feel for what you want to achieve, so that the brainstorming process becomes more focused.
- **Game features** (such as units, weapons, power-ups, and so on) help your game feature a range of different objects that the player needs to collect or use at certain points during gameplay. How can a player get them, how many do they need? The list of questions can go on and on depending on how granular you want to be, but these are important, especially considering that if you cannot answer them, it is probably time to question their relevance in the game.

Tools and methods for getting ideas out and organizing thoughts

There are many types of applications that readers can use for organizing their ideas, concepts, and ways to keep it all together. Brainstorming is a vital yet messy process. Also, depending on the ability of your team to meet on a regular basis, and how they meet (such as in person or online), can cause a range of problems if you want to keep things organized. The following suggestions offer some strategies for managing this both in a virtual and physical sense, but feel free to use or explore other methods that work for you.

Start pinning with Pinterest

Pinterest (www.pinterest.com) is a great starting place to get some basic ideas of all aspects of your application. In fact, because it is primarily based on images (and their associated content) it is a perfect place for inspiration. You can create an account pretty easily, and then once you're ready to go, it's just a matter of setting up *boards*. You can think of boards much the same as a fridge covered in postcards and magnets from your recent trip. It's a collage of different images all centered on the same thing, and the best part is that they can be private or public, it's up to you. If we have a look at the following screenshot, you can see an example of a board with all of its *pins*. Each pin can be accompanied by a description and links to the website that it is related to. For example, if it's a piece of art, then the image may be located on the artist's website. In addition, you can also add other users to help contribute to the board of ideas! However, they will also need a Pinterest account:

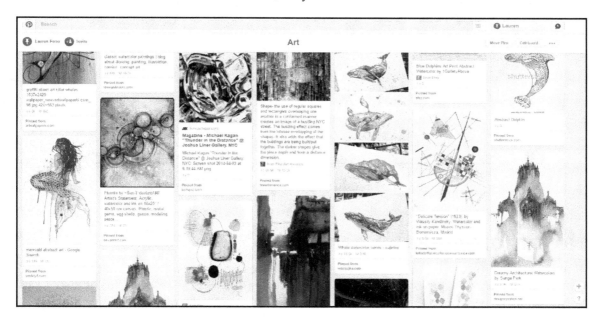

Starting with a fresh slate

Slatebox (`www.slatebox.com`) is a great tool for putting together mind maps. Looking at the following screenshot, we can see an example of the types of mind map that can be created in Slatebox. Slatebox is a free and simple online application that can be used by an individual or shared among a group to create mind maps, as basic or complex as needed:

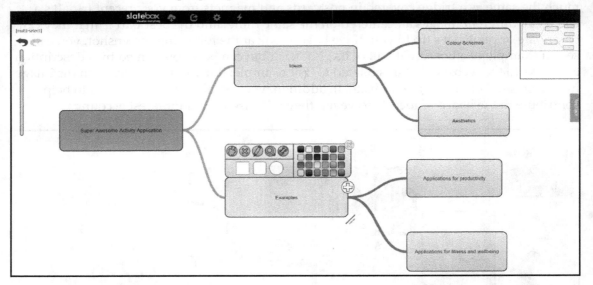

An overview of how SlateBox which comes with a range of different brainstorming nodes and connecting ideas with an example of the toolbox

Never forget with Evernote

Never miss taking a note, writing down a thought, idea or taking a picture that relates to your project with this application, Evernote (`www.evernote.com`). Not only this, it also syncs with Google Drive, making it ideal for being a great collaborative platform. Since it is a mixed-media platform, it also makes it a perfect on-the-go brainstorming tool that can then be reviewed later by your whole team. This means that you can have *distance* brainstorming sessions, where everyone collates ideas on their own in a more organic way than a meeting, where ideas do not necessarily come so easily.

Brainstorming activities

There are many different ways to approach brainstorming. It can be in groups or on your own. In the next section is a list of five activities to get the ideas out of your head, on to paper, and turn them into something extraordinary. Remember that the idea with brainstorming is to get what's in your head out and on paper. It's not meant to be perfect, but rather like emptying a box of jigsaw puzzle pieces. It's only after you begin to sift through them that you know what is useful.

Spinning the wheel of randomness

If you're stuck for ideas to begin with, Andrew Bosley's *The Brainstomer*, `http://andrewbosley.weebly.com/the-brainstormer.html`, which is shown in the following screenshot, is a nifty tool to get some creative juices flowing. There are many different ways to approach The Brainstormer; you could begin with a story that is based on the three elements, or allow each of the three elements to inspire a part of the gamified experience. For example, the first wheel could reveal something about the concept of the game. In this instance, *Fish out of water* could build on the idea of *trying something new*. The second wheel could reveal something about the environment, for example, you need to explore a perfect world (free from zombies!) and to maintain it, you must maintain a healthy habit.

Lastly, the third wheel could reveal a potential character, such as the player his or herself, or a character from the game. For example, the player may have to meet a wizard who needs your help to keep the utopian world from becoming dystopian:

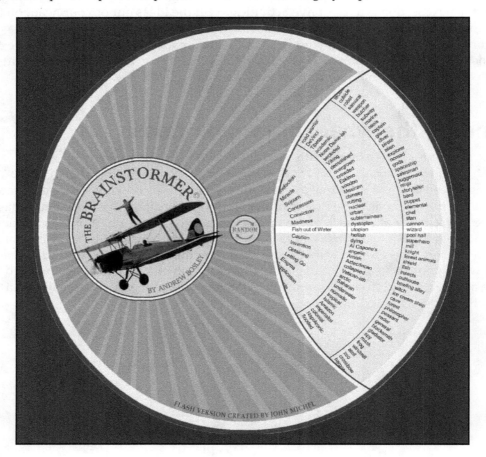

Getting in and among it

The first thing that you should do is find and play as many gamified applications that are related to the topic or concept of yours. Some things to keep in mind are as follows:

- Look at what other types are currently available.
- Look at their feedback. This will usually give you an indication of what has gone right or wrong. Then from this, you can gain some insights about the way you should approach the design of your own application.

- Make notes about everything such as the colors (are there consistent ones).

Game on with Gamicards

Gamicards is a great start for brainstorming ideas in the very beginning and seeing how you can play around with different game elements and mechanics with an idea that you might have. You can incorporate your ideas from other brainstorming activities to get your idea gamified! All it takes is a little imagination and the possibilities are endless.

If we have a look at the following screenshot, the hexagonal shape allows you to build different structures to organize your ideas in a meaningful workflow. Furthermore, they are not only used as just a brainstorming tool. In fact, not only do they support you during the design process, but they also test the gamification infrastructure of your application. By doing this, you can check to see if you are still heading towards the goals that you have in mind:

You can buy them at player26.com, and for you there is a special discount. Send an e-mail to order@player26.com with proof of purchase of this book to get a discount.

 Some other great brainstorming cards and applications that can work in parallel with Gamicards include the Deck of Lenses by Jesse Shell (tinyurl.com/DeckOfLenses) and Grow-a-game (www.valuesatplay.org/grow-a-game-overview).

The great exchange

This activity works by getting each person in a group to write down five ideas. Once they have finished, they then swap their piece of paper with the person next to them, and then they elaborate on each of these five ideas. Then, they pass it to the next person, and so on. This continues until everyone in the group has added something to each other's starting five ideas. Of course, you can continue to exchange the ideas for however long you wish. At the end, the group goes around and discusses each idea and how it has developed, and from that, refines the ideas for the overall project. Remember, your ideas don't have to be confined to realistic concepts. Blue-sky thinking, anything and everything should be written down.

Getting moody with mood boards

Mood boards are a great way of getting the *look and feel* of what you want your game to be like. Mood boards include images of anything and everything from the UI, to characters, color schemes, and so on. Some ways to begin mood boards include the following:

- Take pictures everywhere and anywhere of things that inspire you or give you some kind of idea about your game. Keep a note of them.
- Begin with a large image that captures your overall theme and then add smaller images around it that help to build and add to the theme. For example, you might start with a large image of someone running, and the surrounding images relate to products that are associated with your target audience such as shoes, watches, and so on. You might also add images of color schemes that relate to the image. For example, bright and bold colors appear to create a fun and vibrant atmosphere.
- Remember, mood boards don't have to be digital. Find cutouts from magazines, print outs, and so on. Create a space within the work area that people can contribute to. Having an *open space mood board* can be a great way for people to reflect before contributing, but make sure that with each image, there is an explanation to provide some context.
- Ask someone who is not part of the project to give you feedback about your mood board to see if they also *feel* the mood that you're trying to create. Sometimes we can get so caught up that we forget to take a few steps back from what we are doing.

A great resource for this is Pinterest. You can even add other people to collaborate on the board with you, how awesome is that?

Creating the ideal ideation sessions

So, you have an idea, but what about the opinions of people who could be your potential consumers? Ideation sessions can be run both in-group and out. The effectiveness of running one with both is that you get a better insight about what consumers may actually want and even think about your idea that you may not necessarily would have thought to be the case. For example, in your group ideation session, you want to add some cool coupon retrieval system that users can access after a certain period. However, running the ideation session with members of your potential consumer group reveals that they don't want to have to wait to unlock such features, and if this is the case, then they probably won't use the application. Some things to keep in mind when running an ideation session are as follows:

- Have a clear focus of what you want to achieve but don't let it rule the session. You want to create a relaxed atmosphere where the ideas flow, but at the same time you want to remain focused. It's just about maintaining a balance. Feel free to experiment with different things such as whiteboards, easels, and even Lego!
- Have a varied mix of people as part of the group: ages, demographics, gender, and so on. The more varied the group, the more varied the feedback. Remember that the world is a diverse place, and so will your consumers be!
- Start with a no-restriction brainstorming session. Get all of your participants to say anything and everything that comes to mind based on the topic of the session. Then, refocus the ideas, while eventually filtering out the general ones and refining the ones that have the most impact. Then once you are done, choose around three and detail them. By this point, everyone should be on target and the discussions will become more concentrated.
- Take care of them! Remember that these people are offering you their time, in exchange for a great product that you will then profit from. It goes without saying, but it is important to remember this. Keep them engaged, and if you can see that the atmosphere is tense, try some ice-breaking games. Give them praise for their contributions. Of course, if your budget allows, provide them with some snacks and beverages, especially if they will be there for a while. A little goes a long way.

- Keep in touch with your participants. Not all of the great ideas come at a specific moment. You never know, a participant might think of something fantastic after they have left and you don't want that idea going to waste, so not only provide them with your contact details, but also follow up after the session.

 Don't get too attached to your early ideas. Usually, the first one or two and sometimes even tenth idea are the worst. When brainstorming, write down anything and everything. It's not meant to be perfect, it's meant to be raw and out there.

Implementing a brainstorming tool in Unity to shuffle ideas

This section will teach us how to use Unity as a faithful companion during the developing stage. The code presented here is not intended for a real purpose, but rather to show Unity within another perspective and learn how to use editor scripts. As a result, the only limit will be your imagination.

In this chapter, we discussed the importance of brainstorming in order to develop a concept for our application. In particular, we have seen that sometimes one of the key points in brainstorming is to mix ideas in a random order, since a new perspective could arise.

Now, our goal is to use Unity to create a small brainstorming tool by implementing an editor script. In particular, there will be a text area where it will be possible to insert different ideas (one for each line). Also, there will be a button that extracts one of these ideas at random and displays it in a box below. This is a rough overview of how our project will work:

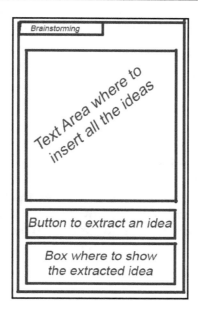

Making a new friend with editor scripts

Unity supports scripts that can extend its functionality. In order to use this kind of script, they need to be inside a folder named `Editor`. So, if we don't have it in our project, let's start by creating one. Right-click on the **Project** panel, and then **Create | Folder**. Of course, don't forget to rename it `Editor`! It's not just a matter of order, but Unity requires this.

Creating an editor script

There are many kinds of editor script. However, in this book we will see only the main one: *creating a new window*.

Inside our `Editor` folder, let's create a script, as usual, by right-clicking and then **Create | C# Script**. We can rename it `BrainstormingTool`.

Double-click to open it.

This is the general class that Unity creates:

```
using UnityEngine;
using System.Collections;
```

```
public class BrainstormingTool : MonoBehaviour {

  // Use this for initialization
  void Start () {
  }
  // Update is called once per frame
  void Update () {
  }
}
```

As we can see, it derives from **MonoBehaviour**. The editor script should not be derived from this class, but from special ones dedicated to extend the editor. In this instance, we will use the **EditorWindow** one. Furthermore, we don't need the `Start()` and the `Update()` functions anymore, so we can remove them. However, to use the **EditorWindow** class we also need to import the Unity Editor library by adding to the beginning of our script the following `using` statement:

```
using UnityEditor;
```

Now, our class should look like the following:

```
using UnityEditor;
using UnityEngine;
using System.Collections;

public class BrainstormingTool : EditorWindow {

}
```

Opening a new editor window

In the next step, we need to create a function that can create our window containing our brainstorming tool. We can name it `showWindow()`. Inside, we need to use the `GetWindow()` function to get the window created by this script. So, as a parameter, we pass `typeof BrainstormingTool`. We can write the following:

```
public static void ShowWindow() {
    //Show existing window instance. If one doesn't exist, make one.
    EditorWindow.GetWindow(typeof(BrainstormingTool));
}
```

However, there is no way to call this function from Unity so far, even if it is `public`. Therefore, we need to add a context menu above the function, which will create a new entry in the toolbar of Unity, as follows:

```
// Add menu item named "Brainstorming Tool" to the Window menu
[MenuItem("Window/Brainstorming Tool")]
public static void ShowWindow() {
    //Show existing window instance. If one doesn't exist, make one.
    EditorWindow.GetWindow(typeof(BrainstormingTool));
}
```

As a result, if we save the script, we will be able to have access to our tool, as shown here:

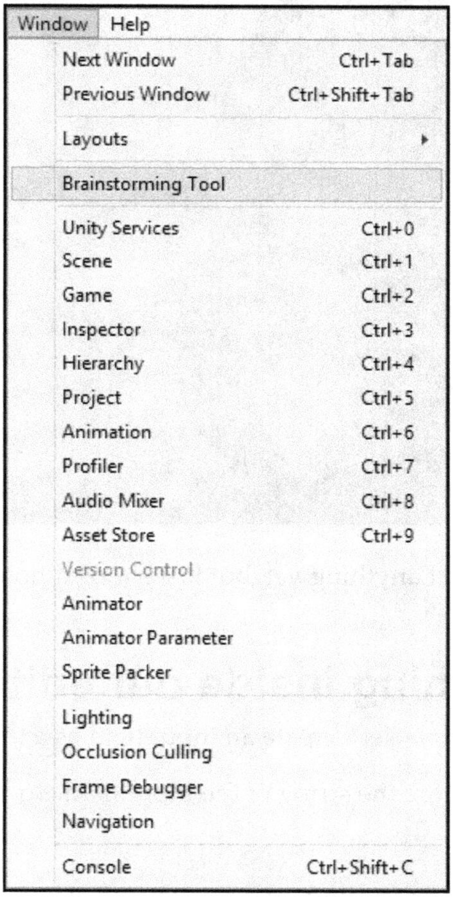

Window	Help	
	Next Window	Ctrl+Tab
	Previous Window	Ctrl+Shift+Tab
	Layouts	▶
	Brainstorming Tool	
	Unity Services	Ctrl+0
	Scene	Ctrl+1
	Game	Ctrl+2
	Inspector	Ctrl+3
	Hierarchy	Ctrl+4
	Project	Ctrl+5
	Animation	Ctrl+6
	Profiler	Ctrl+7
	Audio Mixer	Ctrl+8
	Asset Store	Ctrl+9
	Version Control	
	Animator	
	Animator Parameter	
	Sprite Packer	
	Lighting	
	Occlusion Culling	
	Frame Debugger	
	Navigation	
	Console	Ctrl+Shift+C

Once we click on it, our window will be empty:

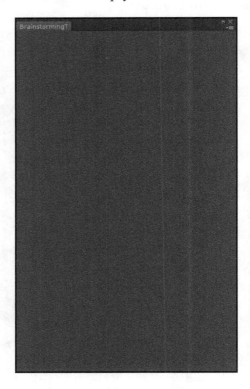

In fact, we haven't implement anything yet, but just showed how to open the window.

Drawing something inside our editor window

Just to get used to editor scripts, let's create an input field as a test.

We first need a variable to store the string of the input field. So, we can write the following:

```
string testString;
```

Then, in order to draw something within the window, we have to use the OnGUI () function. In particular, we use the EditorGUILayout class and the TextField() method. So, let's write the following:

```
void OnGUI() {
    testString = EditorGUILayout.TextField(testString, "TextField");
}
```

If you save the script, and then open your window in Unity, it should look like the following:

Great, not bad so far! But let's go further with the next section.

Adding a scrollable text area

Now it's time we get started with our brainstorming tool. To begin, we want to create the area where you will be able to insert your ideas, one for each line. In particular, we need a private variable for the scrolling, to keep track of where the scroll bar is in each frame, and a string to store the text area. So, erase the variable from the previous section, and instead add the following two:

```
Vector2 scroll;
string ideas = "My first Idea";
```

Then, let's completely rewrite the `OnGUI()` function. To improve the aesthetics, we first add a label with the text `Ideas`. Then we start our scrollable view in the window, and we add the text area. Finally, we close the scrollable view:

```
void OnGUI() {
    GUILayout.Label("Ideas", EditorStyles.boldLabel);

    scroll = EditorGUILayout.BeginScrollView(scroll);
    ideas = EditorGUILayout.TextArea(ideas,
GUILayout.Height(position.height - 30));
    EditorGUILayout.EndScrollView();
}
```

As a result, the following screenshot shows how our brainstorming tool should appear so far:

Now, we are close to achieving what we want!

Inserting a button and implementing the shuffle function

At the bottom of our text area, we want a button to extract one of the ideas. So, at the bottom of our `OnGUI()` function, we need to insert a button. However, as with all the GUI functions in Unity, the buttons should be inserted in an `if` statement, to trigger what should be done once the button is pressed. So we can add the following:

```
if (GUILayout.Button("Extract")) {
    //Button Trigger
}
```

As a result, we will have the button, but nothing would happen if it was pressed. Therefore, let's implement the shuffle functionality.

To begin, we need to have another variable, an array of strings to store all our single ideas. Then, we need a string variable in which to store the extracted idea. At the end, our variables should be as follows:

```
Vector2 scroll;
string ideas = "My first Idea";
string[] ideasArray;
string extractedIdea;
```

Inside the `if` statement of the button, we need to split the ideas string into single ideas to store in `ideasArray`, and then to get one of those at random to store in the `extractedIdea` variable, by using the `Random.Range()` function. In fact, the range should be from zero to the length of the array (since the maximum is exclusive). As a result, this will be our code:

```
if (GUILayout.Button("Extract")) {
    ideasArray = ideas.Split('\n');
    extractedIdea = ideasArray[Random.Range(0, ideasArray.Length)];
}
```

Again, save the script, and see what we have accomplished so far:

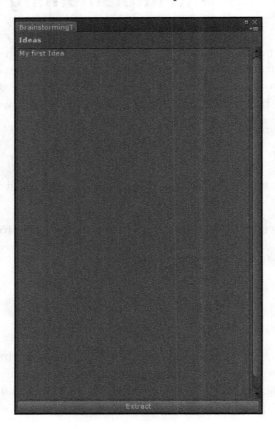

It is important to note that since we have other elements, the scroll bar is now visible. In this case, we only have the button, after the scroll view. However, when we press the button, nothing happens, just like in the following screenshot:

This is because we do extract ideas, but there are no components to show the extracted idea. But that's okay, because we're about to learn how to do that in the next section.

Showing the extracted idea

After the `if` statement with the button, we need to show the extracted idea. For aesthetic purposes, we can separate our window with another label, as follows:

```
GUILayout.Label("Extracted Idea", EditorStyles.boldLabel);
```

Then, we add a `HelpBox` area that will show the extracted idea, by using the `extractedIdea` variable:

```
EditorGUILayout.HelpBox(extractedIdea, MessageType.None);
```

As a result, this is our final `OnGUI()` function:

```
void OnGUI() {
    GUILayout.Label("Ideas", EditorStyles.boldLabel);

    scroll = EditorGUILayout.BeginScrollView(scroll);
    ideas = EditorGUILayout.TextArea(ideas,
GUILayout.Height(position.height - 30));
    EditorGUILayout.EndScrollView();

    if (GUILayout.Button("Extract")) {
        ideasArray = ideas.Split('\n');
        extractedIdea = ideasArray[Random.Range(0, ideasArray.Length)];
    }

    GUILayout.Label("Extracted Idea", EditorStyles.boldLabel);
    EditorGUILayout.HelpBox(extractedIdea, MessageType.None);
}
```

Save the script, and come back to Unity. Now, open our **Brainstorming Tool**. It should look like the following:

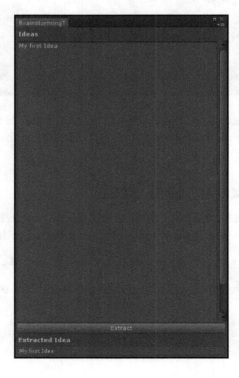

Testing our brainstorming tool

Now, we are ready for the final step-testing. Don't forget to do it, especially before using it. In fact, we need to be sure that there aren't bugs. So, let's insert some random ideas in the text area, one for each line, as shown in the following screenshot:

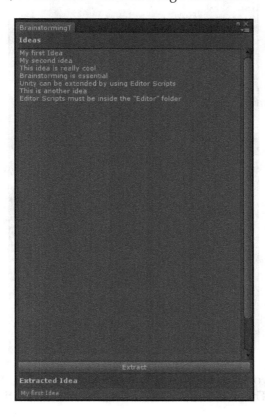

Now, press the button and see which idea has been extracted:

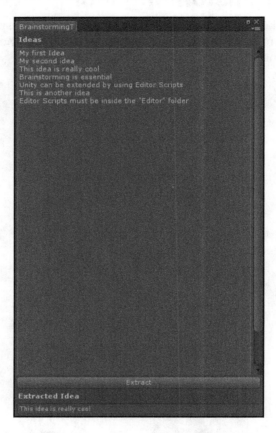

It looks like everything works as it should. You can keep pressing the button to see a different idea extracted. The more ideas you insert, the more effective the tool will be.

 If you need to remove one of the ideas, don't worry. You can just erase the line of the idea you don't want to have anymore. Remember, removing ideas is part of the brainstorming process, so don't be afraid to do it!

Summary

Well, that's that for this chapter! Overall, we looked at how to generate ideas for various game projects. We looked at different brainstorming tools to help make the brainstorming process easier and more manageable. Next, we looked at different methods of brainstorming to get the best ideas out and to also help inspire the creation of new ones. Then, we looked at how to create a randomized idea generator in Unity, which can be also repurposed in many different ways. In fact, we explored and learned how to create an editor script to use Unity not only to produce something for the final user, but also to help us during the creation process. In particular, we learned more about the `EditorWindow` class and how it is possible to use different `EditorGUI` elements to achieve powerful layouts with just a few lines of code.

In the next chapter, we will begin with an introduction to the project that we will create during the rest of this book. We will look at various methods of prototyping. In addition, we will also look at implementing basic navigation into Unity. We will do this with a preliminary mock-up that will form part of the project.

5
Sculpting the Conceptual Beast

Having a hard copy of the application that you have in mind can help you avoid a lot of restructuring and recoding later. Therefore, this chapter introduces a series of tools to get you creating a physical prototype of your application. At this stage, the reader will get an idea about how to test the application with its target audience so that they avoid wasting time and programming resources later in the process. This will also extend what you have done in Chapter 4, *Organized Chaos – Getting Ideas Out of Your Head and on to Paper*, but adding more functionalities.

The list of topics that will be covered in this chapter are as follows:

- At the beginning of this chapter, *Creating a Game Design Document* looks at creating a document that explains your game in more detail. The idea of this document is to provide a guide to you and other members of your team during the development process. It is also useful when trying to contain the scope of the overall project during not only the development but also prototyping and iterative stages.

- Next, *Creating a prototype – what you'll need* will look at a range of considerations that need to be made during the prototype stage and how they all affect the design of your prototype and future development of your game.

- We will then look at *Methods of prototyping*, which examines how to create a prototype based on two popular methods–rapid and paper prototyping.

- In the penultimate section, *Tools for prototyping in Unity* explores the different features of Unity that allow us to easily and quickly set up a prototype of our game or application. Which we will then learn how to implement in *Getting basic core concepts into Unity*.

- Lastly, we will conclude this chapter with *Revising the prototype*, which explains how to revise the final prototype and how to test, iterate, and then take it further.

Creating a Game Design Document

So now, you might have a vague idea about what kind of game you might want to design. If you don't, that is fine for now. This is where we will begin to craft what is known as the **Game Design Document (GDD)**. The point of a GDD is to provide everyone within the game development team with a go-to guide for the game's overall design.

Things that you will want to include in your GDD are the following:

- **Game overview**: What is your game about? Think of it like a more detailed elevator pitch. Someone reading this must be able to get a good understanding of what your game is about and what the player will do. Overall, this will be about 1-2 pages in length. In this section, you will want to also state your aim, objectives, and the outcomes of your gamified application.
- **Core game description**: What is your game in more detail? You can take each point from the overview and elaborate on it in more detail. For instance, your aim is to rescue a princess from the Castle of Ra. This part explains how Ra is the long-lost friend of the princess's father, the king, who tried to kill Ra. You might also want to describe the type of genre that your game will be.
- **Demographics/Audience**: Who are you intending this game for? Where are they from, and are certain ages not allowed to play it (for example, is it for 18+)? This is where you define your demographics and ultimately the target audience for your game. You can also refer to `Chapter 2`, *Who or What Am I? Understanding the Player*, if you want to know more specific considerations about your users.
- **Art/Design**: If you're creating a wonderful mood board depicting the aesthetics for various aspects of your game, this is the place to put it in. Also, with a brief description that somehow explains the intention. For example, you might have a bunch of images from an abandoned warehouse that is the inspiration for the UI and not the actual level itself. Explanations are everything! Ideally, you want to have more refined art that you have created in this section that helps to describe the aesthetic vision and direction of your game.
- **Story**: The overarching narrative drives your gameplay. It can be something as simple as you are the master of some magical deck of cards from various faraway lands or something more intricate, such as our story about Ra and the king. This is where more complex details are revealed to provide substance and explanation for the overall game and gameplay.
- **Characters**: Who the player is and who they will meet along the way are important, especially if they are important parts of the story. Even if there is only one character and that is the player, who they assume the role of and how this is explained in the game is clarified here.

- **Environment**: Is the environment based on reality, augmented reality, or is it purely fictional? The environment is explained in more detail and which parts of it that the player can and cannot go. In this section, it could also be useful to develop a rough map of the environment. The last thing that you could also consider is that the environment doesn't necessarily mean majestic landscapes, or city skylines; the environment is where the user will spend most of their time interacting. Therefore, if you have a 2D gamified application that targets fitness, your environment could be the real world, or the application itself.
- **Features/gameplay**: What kind of cool things can the player do, and how can they do it? This section covers all the different kinds of interaction that the player can perform during gameplay. You can refer to `Chapter 1`, *The Anatomy of Games* for more details about game elements and mechanics.
- **Audio (music, specially effects)**: Audio can really make an experience something memorable. This doesn't necessarily imply something positive either. If you have a really beautifully designed application and every time the player interacts with a certain part of it, some horrendous sound plays, they will want to turn it off, and let's hope that if it is that bad, there is an option to mute it! The same goes for background music. That is where the types of audio that will feature in the game are described and accompanied with examples.
- **UI**: The UI is extremely important, especially how it delivers information to a player at all moments of gameplay. How it looks, how the player interacts with it, and how it responds to interaction (for example, if it takes the player to another part of the game) can be explained here.
- **Time Line**: Ideally, the project needs an end date. That way, milestones can be set and work can be completed by certain dates. Otherwise, the project could go on and on and on.

Of course, this is just a suggested structure. If you are also going to be developing something to pitch commercially say to a publisher, then it will need to include things such as the following:

- **Market analysis**: Market analysis examines what is out there, competition, comparisons with other similar games, and so on. For example, if you're creating a game similar to Candy Crush, you might look at games such as Bejeweled and see how they are performing, what kind of features they have or haven't got, and how successful one is compared to the other, and much more.
- **Technical analysis**: Here, we look at the technical details in more detail, such as the technology used, the types of technical risks that need to be taken (if any), the types of resources that are needed, alternatives, and so on.

- **Legal analysis**: Legal issues can include anything from copyrighted material, licensing of certain software, fees, and also if any types of contract, non-disclosure agreements, and so on need to be implemented as part of the project's development, especially for outsourced work.

- **Cost and revenue projections**: The cost that your game is estimated to be and how much it will make are important to anyone you are trying to have invest in your idea. This can include anything from resources to employment costs, marketing, hardware, and software. The big issue here is to ensure that any numbers that are provided (such as cost, resources, and employee estimates) are supported by some sort of reference. For example, saying that the game will cost $100,000 to develop and two-thirds of that is dedicated to marketing might raise some red flags. This is unless you explain that it is because you're hiring some famous actress to do a 10-second advertisement for your game. Transparency is key.

Now, so far we have just scratched the surface of what *can* be in a GDD. Feel free to use, discard, or even add your own sections. There is no right or wrong way to create a GDD, but they all have the same main purpose. This is to explain to anyone, whether your team or someone from the public, what your game is about. The GDD is a constantly changing document; it will get updated, revised, and will change as your game progresses. Therefore, at each stage of the design process, even after meetings where aspects of the game are changed, it is important to make sure that the GDD reflects these changes accordingly. Now with that all sorted, creating a GDD begins with something to create it in. There are many ways to do this, and we will look at three. A great article that is worth checking out about GDDs can be found at `http://www.gamasutra.com/view/feature/3384/the_anatomy_of_a_design_document_.php`.

Google Drive

Google Drive (with Google Docs) is probably the easiest way to go about creating a GDD, especially if you have a number of people within your group. The benefit of using Drive is that you can keep everything in one place (even with an offline backup if you install the application). It's free and simple to set up: all you need is a Google account. One of the benefits with Drive is that you can not only share the files and/or folders, but you can control who accesses it and what kind of access that they have (for example, edit, read, download, and so on), as well as see changes that are made. The great part of this is that users have the ability to revert to previous versions of the document, in the event something happens. Lastly, a range of different applications are available that we can see in the following screenshot, such as presentation and spreadsheet software:

Word (and Microsoft Office)

Using Word (especially) with Dropbox is another good choice. It already has a bunch of preloaded paragraph styles so that managing sections is a bit easier. It is also less complicated than Google Drive when it comes to working without an Internet connection. Unlike Google Drive, it isn't free, so you will have to purchase a license to use it, if it didn't already come pre-installed with your device. There are also a number of ways that you can have access to Word through either purchasing the product or buying a subscription.

An example of Word can be seen in the following screenshot with its paragraph styles set up (on the right):

InDesign

Now, for those who are extremely into design and have the patience to set up paragraph styles, among *other things*, then InDesign is a great design tool. Despite this, it makes setting up the aesthetics of your document a dream, especially if you want to then show your GDD around or even make it available to the end user as part of the *development process*. InDesign offers many features, a lot more than Word or Google Docs, but requires a bit of knowledge of document processing applications, and terminology.

The only downside to using InDesign is that it doesn't have a sharing capability, so it is best used with some sort of version control program if you are planning on sharing the document on something such as Dropbox. We can see an example of the InDesign interface in the following screenshot:

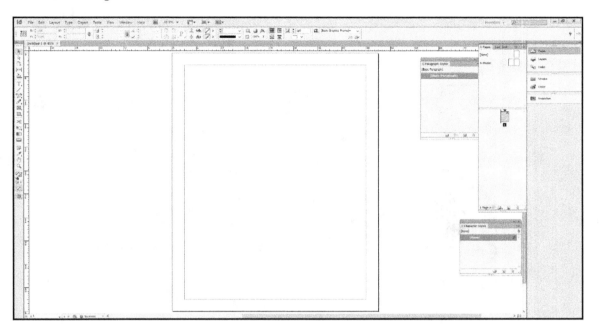

Each of these three programs is fantastic to use. Ultimately, it depends on what you want to achieve in the end. If you want something that keeps everyone on the same page, that is quick, simple, and something that everyone has access to, then Google Drive would be the suggested way to go. If just one or two people are managing the document, then Word is a good option. If you want to publish the GDD at a later date, whether online, printed, or even as something to show prospective publishers, then InDesign is a nice way to go.

Creating a prototype – what you'll need

Now, whether you have an idea in mind about what you want to create or not, here are some basic ideas and tools to get you started. Of course, these are suggestions; there are many, many different ways to create prototypes. For now, use the information on the following pages as a primer, a set of training wheels, until you start to get used to the development process. Make sure that you have some of the items shown in the following image so you can get all the ideas out onto paper!

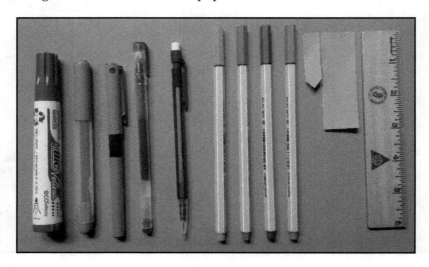

Gathering your humans

The first thing you will need are people to create the prototype. People come in many shapes, forms, talents, and so on, so you want a great bunch of cool people to work with. Even if it's just yourself, that's fine too. The main thing here is to be *crystal clear* about what each person in the development process is responsible for. For example, you might have two programmers in your group, which is great. But make it clear that programmer #1 is responsible for implementing the UI and programmer #2 is responsible for the database. If people have a clear idea of their purpose, they spend less time trying to figure it out, and in the long run, the development of the prototype can be more efficient.

Having a plan!

You now have a group, but before you start getting into developing the initial prototype, think about *what* you want, and *when* you want it done by. Ask yourself questions such as what does the prototype need to include, and how are you going to evaluate the success of it? A prototype answers a question about the game. For example, is it to test the effectiveness of adding additional weapons, or whether or not the player needs to have certain information presented to them all the time during gameplay? Of course, these are basic questions, and games can have more than one question that the prototype needs to answer. The main point here is that there *is* a question that lays down the whole point of the prototype.

Setting a date

This is one of the most important resources of game development. Do you have a day, a couple of weeks, or a few months to create the prototype? You need to set a number of dates. You will need a start and finish date, but also milestones, feature freezes (when no more features are added to prototype). If, during the process, you find that you are running out of time, need more time, or even finish earlier than expected, ask yourself why. If you need more time, what is the reason? Is it because something isn't working, or is it because there are too many things to implement within the timeframe? The same can also be said for if you finish early. Reflect on each part and whether or not it answers the questions, or even if it raises more.

Scoping it out

What do you need to build, and what *is possible* within the limits of the initial prototype? Will you create a demo level with different functionalities that the player will have throughout the game? Is the prototype a preliminary version of a level or part of a level? What needs to be included or excluded to determine if it is valuable to the end product? During the process, it is easy to get lost among it all and think of a cool feature and then begin to implement it. If this happens, then STOP. Review the plan, and only add the essentials. This super cool feature that you want to add now can be done later, if it is still relevant to the overall game.

Keeping it short and to the point

Keeping it to the point and not *perfect* is what you need to keep in mind throughout the whole process. Make it your mantra and don't get attached! One of the worst things that can happen when you're creating a game is that you get attached to an idea that you really like. As a result, you develop something with *tunnel vision* and tend to avoid new and even better ideas from developing because they somehow impinge on your *best idea ever*.

What's your poison?

This is basically what kind of platform you will use to create your prototype, and what device you will ultimately design on, such as those in the following image. Ideally, if you go digital with a game engine (and other software), you will want to use the one that you will eventually develop in. This is *not* to say that while you are creating your prototype, you should spend hours to perfect it so that it can be used later in the game. It *is* to say that by using the software, while also keeping in mind the target device(s) that you will use for the final product, you will become more familiar with the tools and processes, and an overall sense of how the software works:

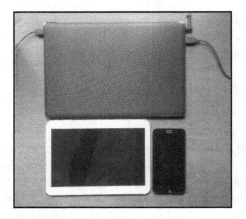

Getting your jam on!

Mini game jams are great ways to get something happening, and it forces you to think within constraints. You can begin with a theme, even restrict yourself to tools for creating a prototype. You can even think of a game jam like a concentrated approach to prototyping. In this case, you dedicate a specific amount of time, which is generally short, to developing a game. Typically, these can last from 24-48 hours, and by the end, you have something rough but functioning. From this point, you can refine it. Just be sure to bring plenty of snacks, beverages, and wear something comfy. It's going to be a long night!

Each year, all around the world many game jams are held with various themes and purposes. One of these is the Global Game Jam, `globalgamejam.org`. Game jams are a great way to get a feel for the overall prototyping and game design process. So, a great tip is to check out ones that are close to you and join in on the fun. It's also a great way to not only develop your game development skills, but also your network, and to most importantly to have fun! Another great example aside from the Global Game Jam is Ludum Dare, `www.ludumdare.com`.

Failing is an option

Don't worry if you don't get it right from the beginning. Chances are you won't in any case. So, expect to fail and expect it often. This may sound like some harsh words, but ultimately, if we got it perfect the first time around then prototyping would be redundant. So, go crazy, take risks, be bold, and most importantly, experiment!

Touching base

Just because everyone in the group agreed to the timeline and the work doesn't mean that it will be done and on time. This can happen for various reasons: life issues pop up, things are harder than anticipated, and so forth. Keep the communication lines open when developing a prototype, and the chances are that as the deadline is drawing closer, so is the prototype. Don't be afraid to admit you don't know how to do something that you have been assigned or agreed to do. Sitting there doing nothing is not going to make it any easier when it's a week out from the finish line and you haven't done anything, than saying something right from the beginning.

Methods of prototyping

There are many different methods of prototyping a game; in fact, you could probably write a book on it. The two main methods of prototyping are paper and rapid. Each can use a range of different materials, just like in the image below, or you can create it digitally.

Paper prototyping

To put simply, it involves no use of technology and only physical materials. This is what caveman game developers would have used before creating their final games. Paper prototyping includes using primitive resources such as pens, paper, scissors, glue, post-it notes, stickers, and so forth. The idea is to get your basic ideas out and get a more physical visualization, for example, if you're creating a game to encourage workplace productivity. You might reconstruct a portion of your workspace environment and then add various elements such as obstacles (which can be plastic counters) that the player has to overcome during their hourly commute to get coffee. It's also a good way to quickly generate many versions and to make observations about how gameplay is affected if something is added, removed, or changed. The best part is that it involves no code, so before you start pulling your hair out because of bugs or features that didn't quite work the way you thought they did after spending weeks implementing them, you get to rough it out old-school! The following is a list of common items that you can use around your house or find at your local dollar shops for use during paper prototyping sessions:

- Pens, pencils, highlighters
- Erasers (also make great counters)
- Toy money
- Dice
- Bottle caps
- Clothes pegs/pins
- Stones
- Index cards
- Post-it notes
- Colored paper (varying shapes and sizes)
- Glass pebbles

 A fun activity to get you used to the paper-prototyping process is to *reverse engineer* popular games such as Pac-Man, Space Invaders, or even Donkey Kong. Use a large piece of paper for the ground and draw or print out the characters and even some of your own and see how you can modify or *mod* the games into something different.

Rapid prototyping

Just as the name suggests, this encourages a quick turnaround of the prototype from an idea to something a bit more tangible. It draws upon the same principles as discussed in *Creating a prototype – what you'll need*, just within smaller time constraints. The key thing to keep in mind here is that you have to be decisive with your ideas and remain efficient. You will throw away ideas and spend time on things that can be discarded later in the game. The main thing is to identify when to keep going with an idea and when to let go. The easiest way to determine if an idea is worth keeping and working on is to look at it through the perspective of the goals and questions that you set out to achieve with the prototype. If the current part is drifting away from this, then either put it aside until later or discard it completely. Avoid ideas becoming complex and technical, and focus on their functionality and creativity.

Some great books to check out about the game design and prototyping process are as follows:

- *Level Up!: The Guide to Great Video Game Design* by *Scott Rogers*
- *Rules of Play: Game Design Fundamentals* by *Katie Salen*
- *Game Design Workshop: A Playcentric Approach to Creating Innovative Games* by *Tracy Fullerton*

Tools for prototyping in Unity

In the following sections, we will explore the different kinds of tools that Unity offers to develop prototypes. By following these simple steps, you can get basic components into your prototype and get key functionality happening.

Placeholder sprites

One of the best ways to distinguish between different elements in the scene, when we don't have the assets yet, is still visually. In fact, using temporary assets can be a handy and rapid way to understand the general look of the game. Therefore, we can use different shapes and colors.

From Unity 5.3, there is the possibility to have some shapes for sprites built in. You can have access to them by navigating to **Asset | Create | Sprites**. As you can see from the following screenshot, we have different options to choose from:

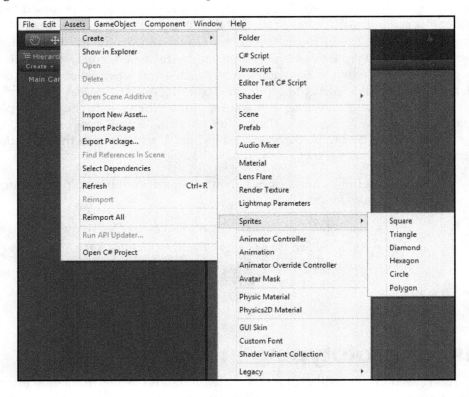

Unity will create some new assets in your **Project** view, as shown here:

They can be then imported into the **Scene** view:

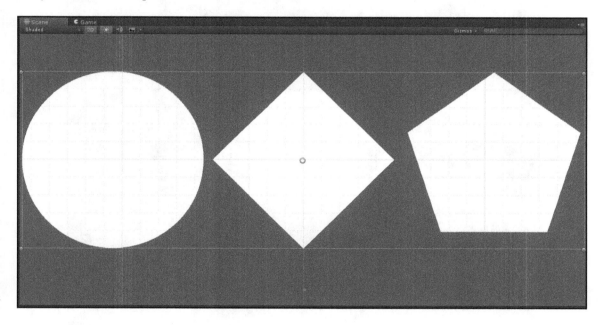

If you need a custom number of edges for your polygon, you can select it in the **Project** panel, and then click on the **Sprite Editor** button in the **Inspector**. You will see the following screen:

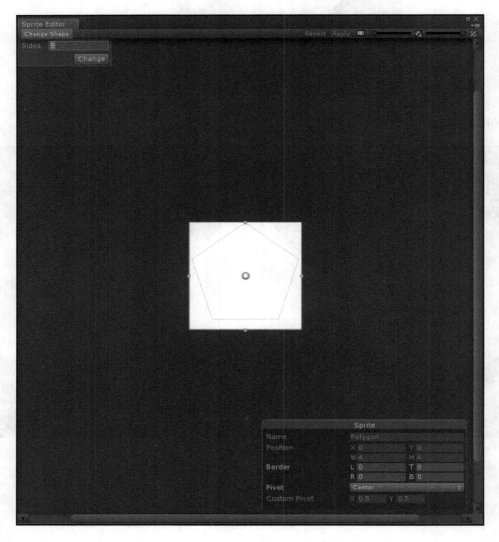

From the top-left corner, you are able to change the number of the edges, and therefore obtain a custom polygon.

Furthermore, if we click on one of them in the **Inspector**, we should see the **Sprite Renderer** component:

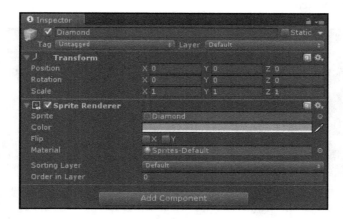

From there, we can change the color variable and assign different colors to our shapes:

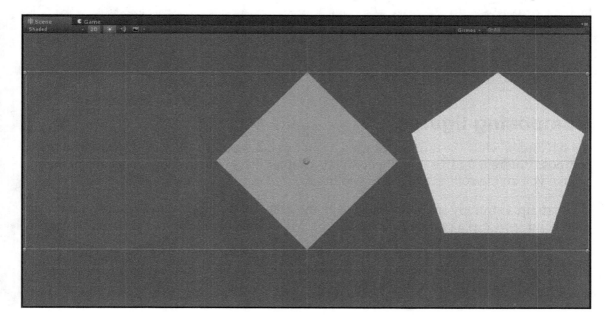

As a result, we will have infinite combinations of colors and shapes. In fact, keep in mind that you can rotate and scale them as well! They should be enough to prototype every 2D game or game-like application:

Composing figures

Even if after a while the number of sprites you can use seems to be limited, you can actually compose different figures from them. In this chapter, I'm going to show you some of them to give you an idea of the endless possibilities.

As a pro tip, I strongly suggest you store all the different figures inside an empty game object and save it as a prefab. As a result, you will be able to quickly use your shapes again.

 You can find a lot more information about using and creating prefabs in Unity in the official documentation that can be found here: `https://docs.unity3d.com/Manual/Prefabs.html`.

Arrow

Creating an arrow is really simple. You just need a rectangle and a triangle. For the rectangle, you can use a square and scale it on one side. Then, place the triangle on top of it. The following screenshot shows how, by highlighting the two polygons with different colors:

Star

In order to create a star, we need two polygons with the same odd number of edges. The result will be a star with double the number of points of each polygon. So, for instance, if we use two triangles that have three points each, we will come up with a star with six points. Instead, if we use pentagons (polygons with five points each), we will have a star with 10 points. As you may understand, we cannot create a star with less than 6 points or with an odd number of edges in this way. However, this method is great to add some more figures to our prototype.

So, once we have decided which polygon to use, just duplicate it with *Ctrl + D* and rotate the clone along the Z-axis by 180 degrees. As a result, you will be able to create all these different stars, which you are free to color as you like:

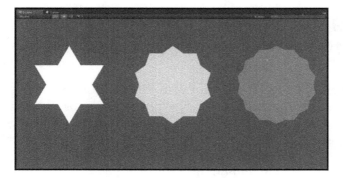

Assets mock-up

With these basic figures, you can also create rapid mock-ups of your assets. For example, you can create a small house, such as the one in the following screenshot:

The house has been created with just ten sprites. The door is a stretched square with a circle for the handle. The windows are just squares; the squares that create the window frame are stretched. Finally, the house is just a big square with a scaled triangle on the top for the roof. By doing all of this, it should show you how easy prototyping is in Unity, and how to create temporary assets that look like the object you intend to represent in your game. Therefore, from now on, free your imagination and create as many assets as you want!

Substituting the temporary assets

Now, we need to briefly go through how to substitute our temporary assets with the final ones once we have them.

If you have placed everything to scale, and your art team (or yourself) has come up with assets that have the same dimensions of the graphics, then substitution is really easy. Just take the temporary asset you have created, such as a triangle, and change the `Sprite` variable in the **Inspector**. On the other hand, as often happens, the assets are sometimes not properly placed, or they need some adjustment to look as they should. However, this process should proceed quickly without many difficulties.

If we have placed a composed asset, such as the house of the previous section, then it is probably inside a game object. In this case, you can erase all of its children (the shapes that compose the object) and add a **Sprite Renderer** to the object. We can achieve this by clicking on **Add Component | Rendering | Sprite Renderer**. Here, you can substitute the `Sprite` variable. Again, you might need some adjustments.

Using labels

Another way to distinguish the objects, and to better communicate your idea, is to include a label with the name of the object.

In Unity, we are able to create them really quickly. Select the object that you want the label on. In the **Inspector**, click on the cube symbol next to the name of the object, as shown here:

As a result, you will see the following menu:

In the first two lines, we see long bars with some colors. If we select one of them, a label with that color and the name of the object will appear in the scene view. This can be seen in the following screenshot:

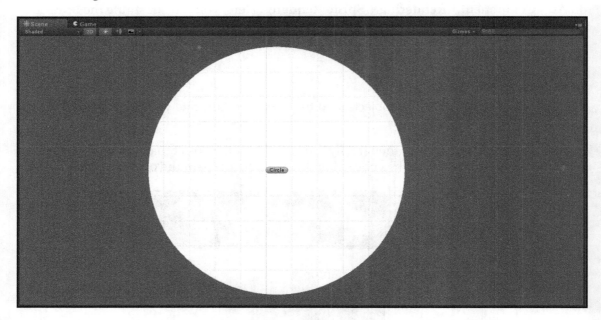

This is a great way to label all the objects in our game, so that even if it is just a circle, it may be our character in a game or a button for an application. Some of you may wonder what the other buttons below are in the previous menu. The little circle allows us to add a small circular icon of that color in the scene view. This is useful if you want to detect an object, or distinguish it without need of a label. An example is shown in the following screenshot with a triangle:

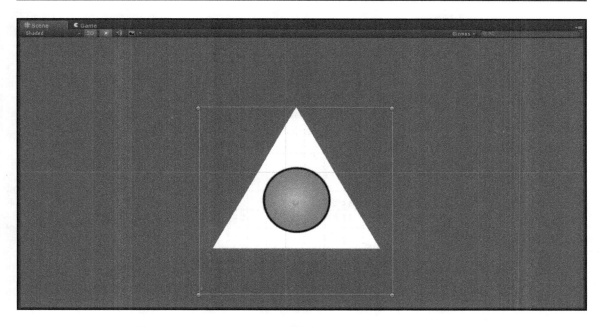

Finally, if we press the **Other** button, then we can choose a custom icon among our assets. Also, it's a great way to place different objects of the same type with the same icon. Personally, the method that I'm more comfortable working with is to use labels because it makes the whole process a lot easier. However, the payoff is to name all the objects correctly in the scene, which is good practice in any case. Therefore, feel free to use the method that you prefer.

Gizmos

One last method we will cover in this chapter is the use of **Gizmos**. Unfortunately, we don't have time to go through this in detail, so we will just scratch the surface to understand why they are so useful. If you are interested in learning more about them, read the official documentation, which can be found at `https://docs.unity3d.com/ScriptReference/Gizmos.html`. Gizmos are icons or drawings inside the scene view that can change at runtime by using scripts. They are really useful during the debug process, but they can also be used to prototype complex movements or animations. In this chapter, we will just limit it to drawing a line.

First of all, create a new script, and rename it `GizmosExampleClass`. Double-click to open it. You can erase the `Start()` and the `Update()` function, since we will not use them.

Add the following variable, which holds a transform that we will use as the ending position of our line:

```
public Transform target;
```

When we deal with Gizmos, we need to implement a special function called `OnDrawGizmos()`. First, we need to check if our target is not null, to avoid reference to an object we don't have. Then, we can decide a color, by assigning the `Gizmos.color` variable. Finally, we can draw a line from the position of our object to the target:

```
void OnDrawGizmos () {
    if (target != null) {
        Gizmos.color = Color.magenta;
        Gizmos.DrawLine(transform.position, target.position);
    }
}
```

Save the script, and create a couple of sprites, for instance, a triangle and a square. Attach the script to the **Square**, and drag and drop the triangle into the target variable, as shown here:

As a result, in the **Scene** view you should see the following (I also added the labels, as in the previous section, for ease of understanding):

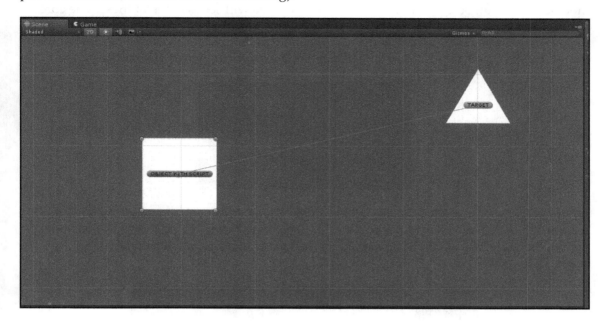

Getting basic core concepts into Unity

So, you have some rough ideas of what you want to do in Unity. You might have a simple mock-up ready and now you want to see how it feels as you navigate through that mock-up. So now, you need to learn how certain navigation systems work within Unity. In this section, we will look at how you can get your mock-up into Unity.

Quick navigation

What happens if we have more than one screen in our game? In this case, we need to simulate the passage from one screen to another without implementing it all. After all, we are just prototyping to see which is the best solution.

So, now you have some rough ideas of what you want to do in Unity. You might have a simple mock-up ready, and now you want to see how it feels as you navigate through that mock-up. This can be done in many ways in Unity, we will see just one of these. The core idea is to include every screen inside an empty game object. Once we have all our screens inside some game objects, it's also useful to rename them in order to understand what they are. At the end, you should have something like the following in the **Hierarchy** panel:

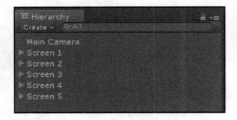

At this stage, we are able to see all of them in the **Scene**, but we don't want this. Therefore, we need to deactivate all of them but one. To deactivate them, just uncheck the little box next to the game object name (**Screen 2**), on the left, as highlighted in the following screenshot:

As a result, we should come up with something like this in the **Hierarchy** panel:

Then, to pass from one screen to another one, just deactivate the current game object and activate another screen. In the previous chapter, we learned about editor scripts. You can implement this switching automatically by using them. Now, we are finished with creating the initial prototype within Unity.

Revisiting the prototype

Unluckily, the story does not finish when we finish the prototype. In fact, the most important part is testing and revisiting the prototype. Of course, as we have seen, while we construct a prototype, we make many decisions, and try to figure out which one fits better. Even failing is allowed to better construct a new prototype. However, even when it seems that it is stable and works as it should, the prototype is not finished yet. The next step is testing the prototype with real users and to get their opinions and thoughts about your prototype.

Testing with the closest people

The first group of people you should use as testers are the people in your team and the families of your team. In fact, these people are easy to reach and probably willing to help you improve your projects. However, there are some considerations to take into account. For instance, they are strongly biased. Therefore, you should be careful. In any case, they will provide you with a solid background when testing with other people that do not know or know only a little of your project.

Testing with external people

Testing with external people is definitely better, but also definitely more difficult. In the first place, they most probably will not be willing to help you without something in return. If you cannot afford to pay them, there are other different options. One of these options is to reward the people with a copy of your application once it is finished. Another could be to add their name to the credit list.

How to test

There are many different ways to test your prototype with people. The simplest way is to just watch testers play around with your application. Techniques that are more sophisticated include questionnaires and measurements of metrics. Playtesting is covered in Chapter 8, *Break, Destroy, and Rebuild – the Art of Playtesting and Iteration*, so be sure to check it out in more detail.

Revisiting your prototype and iterating

Once you have collected all your feedback, it's time to revisit your prototype. Take into consideration all the different feedback you received, and see what it has in common. Try to draw a main direction, and from this abstract direction, create a list of improvements to your application for a specific part of it. You should focus on one part of it at a time. Finally, once you have implemented all the tasks, you need to repeat the entire process and iterate.

> Of course, in this section we have just scratched the surface of testing and revisiting. We will take a deeper look at all these topics in Chapter 9, *Graduating Your Project to Completion*, where we will learn the different techniques through a practical example.

Summary

In this chapter, we covered the concept of a GDD, what it contains, and other things to think about when it comes to explaining the concept of our game. In addition, we looked at what programs to use to create it. Next, we looked at what we need to create a prototype and how to create one. We looked at the different considerations that needed to be covered before beginning a prototype and two popular methods of prototyping known as *paper prototyping* and *rapid prototyping*. Lastly, we looked at tools for prototyping in Unity and revising the prototype, while getting the basic core concepts into Unity. In Chapter 6, *Breathing Life into Your First Creation – Making It Digital!*, we will begin by going over the project that will be developed throughout the remainder of this book. We will set up the project in Unity and implement some features that we have learned about in previous chapters and integrate them with some new features.

6
Breathing Life into Your First Creation - Creating and Importing Assets for Your Application

What is more exciting than to see how we can transform an idea, or collection of ideas into something that we can play, touch, and even interact with? The amazing thing about the world that we live in is that if you can think it, you can create it, *in one way or another*. In this chapter, we will finally start to build our application, and bring it to life! In particular, we cover the following topics:

- To begin this chapter, we will look at *Designing our application,* which focuses on getting our idea out of our head and onto paper.
- Next, *Creating the game elements and An introduction to Illustrator* will guide you through learning the basics of Adobe Illustrator to create basic icons for our application
- The we will look at *Importing the graphics into Unity* so that you can learn how to get the creations we have made in Illustrator into Unity
- We will then learn how to *Import Settings in Unity* and how to set up Unity properly so that the assets we import are ready to go into our application
- To conclude this chapter, we will look at *Importing and* setting *our assets in Unity* to making sure that everything is working as it should and that we are able to have a functioning application for the later chapters of the book

So now, we're going to talk about something exciting, the project that we will create throughout the rest of the book! What kind of project is it, you may be wondering? Well, it's going to be an application that will combine all of the knowledge that you have gained over the last four chapters and start to bring it together. But wait, there's more! We will also be developing some more skills and learn a thing or two along the way. So, get yourself comfortable, you're in for a real treat.

Designing the application

The project that we will be developing is a 2D application for increasing the productivity of an individual. Now, what productivity is related to is relative, so ultimately feel free to associate it with anything from house chores to arriving at work on time. We are leaving it pretty open-ended so it is possible to target various types of productivity and not any single one in particular. It might even be useful to create a mind map such as the following figure to get some ideas flowing. Remember to include any thoughts that you have, because we can fine tune it later:

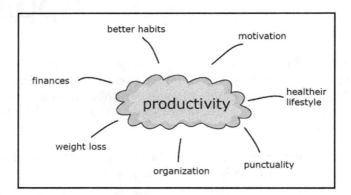

For now, if you can't think of some interesting ideas for your application, I encourage you to go through the previous chapters. For example, maybe it is worth going through some Pinterest boards to look for some cool ideas to create a fitness application. Maybe you already have an idea but would like to create it in a particular way, so it's just a matter of organizing your thoughts. You might even need some help with ways to incorporate game design, and for this I encourage you to play with existing applications to get a feel for different approaches. Therefore, I recommend that you play and play often. Also, as you think of ideas, write them down, sketch them; even rough ideas all help in the later stages of the development. The following are some sketches of the earlier development for the design of this book's application:

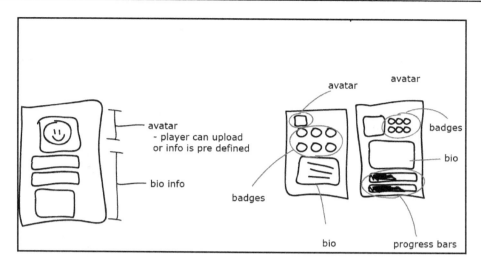

Examples of the application's profile (left) and dashboard (right)

The following figure indicates how a user is able to set a task date within the application. You can see that both the task set date menu (left) and the main menu item **tasks** (right) are featured within the image. Again, these are just the initial stages of design, and we will refine them as we go:

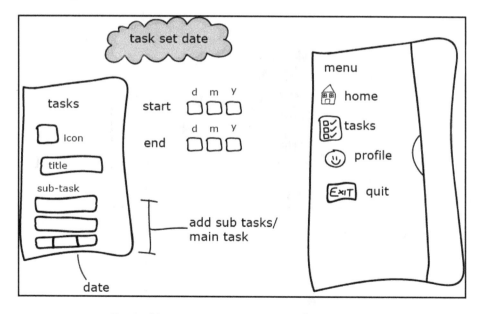

Examples of the task setting menu (left) and main menu (right) of the application.

Creating the game elements

This section will explain to you how to create the various game elements that we will be using for our project. It will guide the reader through various tools and shortcuts in Adobe Illustrator (which can be found at `www.adobe.com/in/products/illustrator.html`) to create each icon. You should keep in mind that Illustrator takes a little time to get used to; therefore, it is worthwhile checking out some basic tutorials to get you started.

Keep in mind that if you are not able to use Illustrator (or some of the alternative software proposed later), you can always find the graphics you need for this book at `player26.com`.

In any case, creating your own graphics adds a personal touch to your application. For this reason, I suggest you at least try to follow the next sections and experiment with the graphics, even if this is your first time.

Adobe Illustrator

Illustrator is a software developed by Adobe Systems and it is used to manipulate **Vector Graphics**:

If you want to know more, or to purchase it, visit this link:

`https://www.adobe.com/products/illustrator.html`

However, there are some free alternatives to Illustrator, such as InkScape (`https://inkscape.org/en/`) or Affinity Designer (`https://affinity.serif.com`). Feel free to choose the one you prefer.

Since we are only going to use basic functionalities, we don't need to have a specific version of any of these programs. In any case, if you can, get the last version of the software that you are going to use.

Vector graphics

If you don't know what a vector image is, continue reading this section; otherwise, feel free to skip it.

The concept of an image that you are most likely used to is the one made out of pixels. These can have different colors, and all of them together create an image. This method is perfect for representing very complex shapes, such as human bodies. In fact, photos are made of pixels. However, the main problem is that they cannot be scaled without losing quality. On the other hand, vector images are not made of pixels, but mathematical formulas/functions that represent the objects. An example of these differences is shown in the following figure:

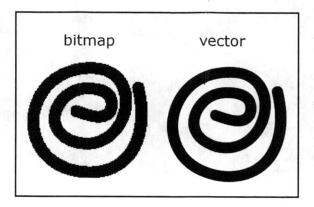

As a result, the computer can keep computing those functions to whatever scale you want, without reducing the quality. The best part is that in order to create vector images, you don't need any math skills; this process is completely handled by the computer. The downside is that it is difficult to represents complex shapes such as human bodies.

So, in saying all of this, if your graphics are made out of geometric shapes (such as triangles, polygons, and so on) or a combination of them, vector images are for sure the best choice. One of the common uses of vector images is for logos.

For these reasons, we are going to use vector images in this chapter.

An introduction to Illustrator

When you open Illustrator, you will see a screen like the following. It looks pretty empty, but there are a few essentials that we will need to set up before we begin making our icons:

One thing to do is to open a few new windows that will be useful later on. They are highlighted in the following screenshot:

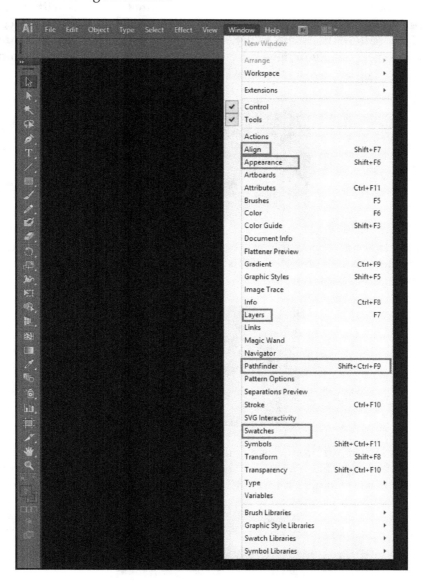

The following are the uses of the highlighted menu options:

- **Align** basically allows us to align and distribute the objects within our scene evenly. This is particularly useful when you want to achieve an effect, such as a striped pattern. It also helps if you want to center objects within your scene either to the objects that you have selected or to your Artboard. You can think of your Artboard as the canvas that you are painting on:

- **Appearance** is responsible for the special effects that we will add later, such as drop shadow or outer glow. This window makes it easier to edit the settings or to remove them from our objects:

- **Layers** are the different parts of the scene. Think of them as sheets that are stacked on top of one another. The layer on the bottom will be behind all the other objects that are on top of it:

- **Pathfinder** (note the shortcut as well) is useful for when we want to merge, add, or subtract shapes from one another:

- **Swatches** are palettes of different colors that we can choose from for this project:

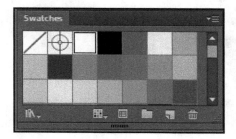

Now that we have opened these windows, it is time to create the project. Select **File** | **New**:

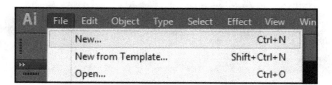

You will be presented with a screen, as shown in the following screenshot, that asks you to create the dimensions of your document. Since we will be creating the background for an application, we will need to assign the following dimensions: 1,080 x 1,920 pixels (or px, which is an abbreviated term, just like cm and mm). The rest of the settings can be left the same; just make sure that the **Color Mode** is set to **RGB** since we will not be printing it, but viewing it on a screen! Lastly, give it a name, and click **OK**:

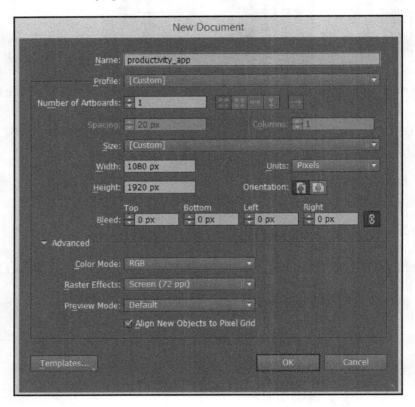

Now, you should have something that looks like the following screenshot. Feel free to rearrange the windows as you want. Make sure, once you have done this, to save your document, navigate to **File | Save**. Keep the settings as they are and save it in a suitable location:

Now that you have the *size* of your application set, we can begin to create the different elements. We will do this within this document so that as we are designing we get a better feel for the size, proportion, and their appearance on screen and within the application's dimensions.

The document setup is pretty straightforward. Once you get used to what everything does and where everything is, the design process will flow a lot faster. Remember that all the windows that we have opened can be moved around so that they are located in places that are more comfortable for you to work with.

Creating badges in Illustrator

As we have already discussed in this book, there are many different ways to create icons within any graphics program. So, choose the program that meets your needs and the one that you are most comfortable with. For the following examples, and for the creation of assets within this book, we will use Adobe Illustrator. We will explore a few different ways to achieve the same thing that cater to both novices and advanced users.

Different icons that are used within the application for this book

Getting all rounded

There are two ways to go about creating rounded corners in Illustrator. One is a redefined shape, the other is an effect. Rounded corners are a nice way to add subtle effects to the overall aesthetic of a UI. They can make things feel less rigid than just using straight edges, and there are many different ways to go about it. We will discuss two ways for creating rounded corners in this section: using the **Shape** tool, which is presented in the following screenshot, or we can create rounded corners by using an *effect*.

Using the Shape tool

For us to begin creating images, we must first select the **Shape** tool, which is located in the **toolbox** menu on the left-hand side in Illustrator. To view more options, simply drag the mouse's cursor over the **Shape** tool, and a small selection screen should appear, as in the following screenshot:

Click anywhere in the scene, and then a pop-up box should appear, as shown in the following screenshot:

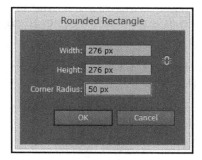

Set the values for the size of the square (or rectangle). If you want the size to be equal on both sides, make sure that the link on the right is selected. If you want to make a rectangle, deselect it. Lastly, enter the amount that you want your corners to be *rounded* in **Corner Radius**; we will use 50 px. Once you are happy, click **OK**. You should have something that looks like the following image:

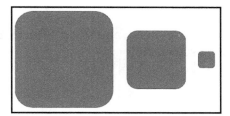

Now, if you want to scale the square up or down, you can do so without creating any distortion, as seen in the following image:

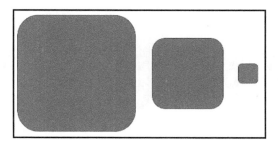

The square has been enlarged (left), original image (center), the square has been made smaller (right)

Using the effect

I recommend using the **Effect** option to achieve rounded corners, mainly because it is less complicated to edit later if you decide that you want your edges to be more or less rounded than they already are. In addition, it also makes it easier to adjust the corners when you are scaling the object up or down.

First of all, you will need to create an object. For this example, we will create a pink square, as shown in the following image:

Next, select your square, go to the top menu, and select **Effect | Stylize | Round Corners...**. You can see this in the following screenshot:

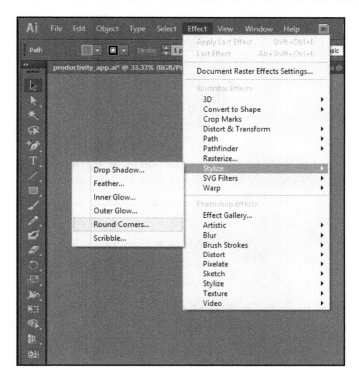

You will see a pop-up menu appear, as shown in the following screenshot, that needs us to enter in a number to determine how *round* our corners will be. Make sure that you check **Preview** so that you can see the effect as you experiment. Choose a value that you are comfortable with, and then click **OK**:

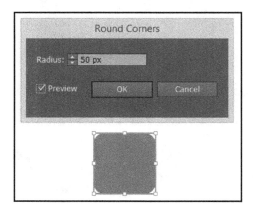

Now you should have a nice rounded square:

However, it is important to keep in mind that as you scale the image up or down, the *roundness* of the edges will change. An example of this can be seen in the following figure:

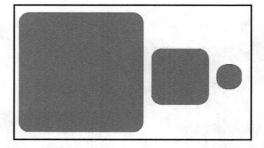

The square has been enlarged (left), original image (center), the square has been made smaller (right)

However, you are able to edit the corners in the the **Appearance** window. We can see the option to edit the **Rounded Corners** in the following screenshot:

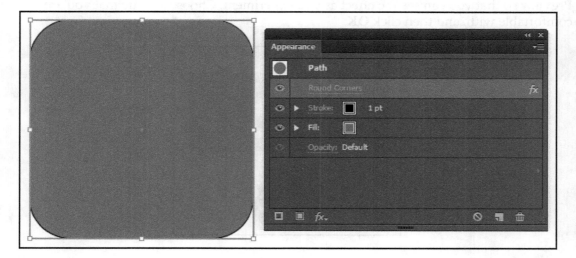

Double-click on the **Rounded corners** option and a pop-up box will appear, as shown in the following screenshot. Make sure **Preview** is selected and then adjust the **Radius** to what you want:

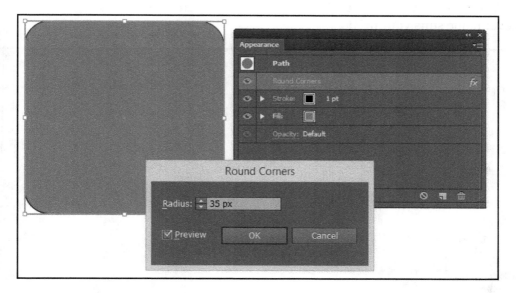

Showing the best of you with badges

Now that we know how to create a rounded square, we will need to create four, which we will use in the application later. To begin, create a new document, and call it `Badges`.

Next, we will need to create four **Artboards**. First, click on the Artboard icon in the toolbox menu, identified as number **1** in the following screenshot. Next, change the height and width to 50 px, identified as number **2** in the following screenshot. Lastly, change the name of the Artboard, identified as number **3**, to something useful, such as task_badge, or whatever name suits your needs:

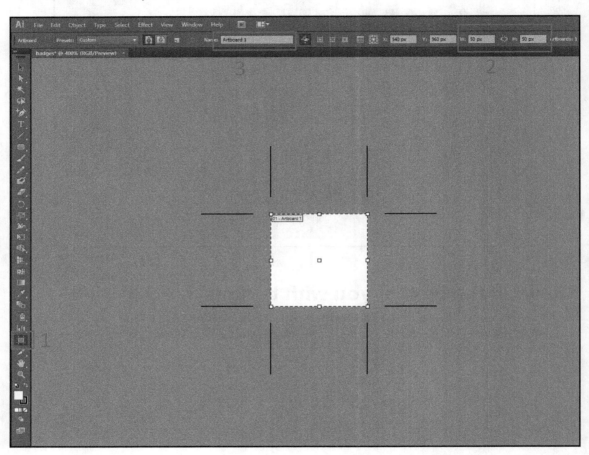

Create a rounded corner square and place it in the middle of the Artboard, as shown in the following screenshot. Feel free to choose any colors that you wish:

Once we have done all this, it is time to create a simple star icon. You can do this by clicking and holding on the shape icon in the toolbox and then selecting the **Star** shape, as shown in the following screenshot:

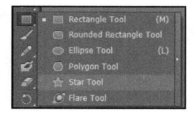

Simply drag your mouse to create your star and then color it as you wish. We chose a golden yellow:

Now, you are free to create any type of icon. They don't even have to be rounded corners; just let your imagination guide you.

Next, we need to export the badge so that it's ready to use in Unity. To do this, select **File | Export**, as shown in the following screenshot:

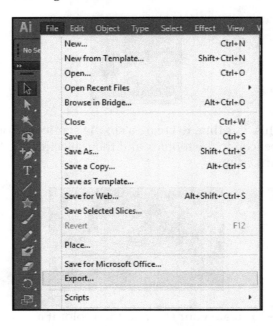

Make sure you give your file a name, that **Use Artboards** is selected, and that you select the file type as `.png`, as shown in the following screenshot:

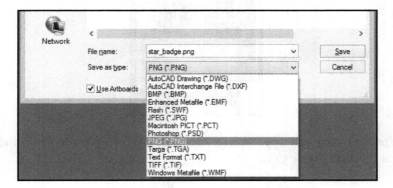

Now, change the resolution to **Screen (72 ppi)** and make sure that the background color is set to **Transparent**, as shown in the following screenshot. Once you are done, click **OK**:

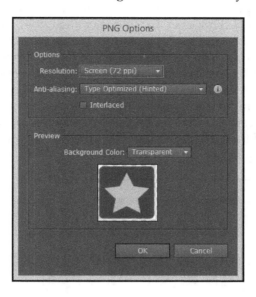

Aiming above the bar

There are many different purposes that bars can serve in a game, from displaying progress to health. They can be in various shapes and forms, just like in the following screenshot:

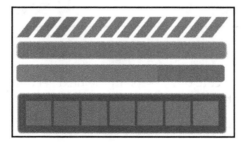

A simple way to create one is using similar techniques to what we did previously with the badge. We can create a rectangle, using either method (**Shape Tool** or **Effect**). Then, we can add different shapes to indicate a segment of progression. We can also add a gradient if we want to! To add segments, it is just a matter of creating smaller squares or rectangles that are smaller than the bar itself and then aligning and distributing them.

Putting it all together with sprite sheets

Creating sprite sheets is a pretty simple process. Sprite sheets are like the sticker sheets that you got when you were a kid. However, in a game context, they can contain every frame of a character's animation, or parts of the UI layout, in such a way that a designer can cut them up and use them within Unity. You can find many online guides to do this, but one of the simplest ways to do this is to create a large Artboard and then copy your icons (once they are finished). Make sure that each element of the icon (such as background, icon image, and so on) are grouped. You can do this by selecting all of the components in the image and then pressing *Ctrl + G* (or *cmd + G* for Mac Os). Once you have your icons on the Artboard and in a group, align, and then distribute them so that the sprite sheet is organized. An example is in the following figure:

We can export this as a unique sheet named `badges-sheet`.

So far, we have seen how to create our assets. In the next sections, we will explore how we can properly import them into Unity in order to achieve exactly what we want.

Importing and setting our assets in Unity

The process of importing assets in Unity is pretty straightforward. However, some tweaks in the settings are needed in order to use the assets for our gamified application. In this section, we will go through the basics of this process, and learn how to import sprites correctly.

Importing assets

In Unity, there are different ways to import assets.

- **From the top menu bar**: Just click on **Assets | Import New Asset...** and a file
  selection menu appears. Then, navigate through your folders and select the file
  that you would like to import.
- **From the Project panel**: Right-click on it and select **Import New Asset...**, a file
  selection menu appears and the asset that you select to import will be imported
  into the folder where you right-clicked.
- **Drag and drop**: From the explorer of your OS, you can just drag and drop the
  files you want into the **Project** panel. In particular, if you drop them into a folder,
  they will be imported into that specific folder.

Of course, the easiest way to import the assets is the last one, and I'll use this. However, just
feel free to use the one that you prefer or suits your needs better.

Import Settings

Once we click on an asset in the **Project** panel, its **Import Settings** appears in the **Inspector**.
They may change with different kinds of asset, but since our application is 2D, we will
mainly use images, and therefore sprites. For instance, let's select **badges-sheet**; we will see
the following in the **Inspector**:

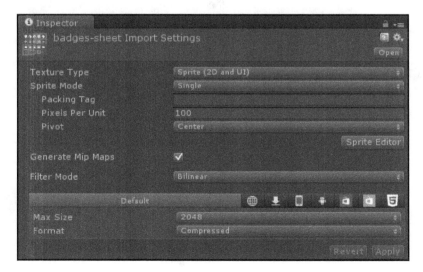

The first option to take into consideration is the **Texture Type**. If we have selected 2D mode when we created the project, it should already be set to **Sprite (2D and UI)**. If it is not, then you need to change this option back to **Sprite (2D and UI)** for all of the assets that you have imported.

If our game is not set in 2D, it could be because we forgot to do so when we created the game, but we can change that. You need to go to **Edit | Project Settings | Editor**. If you go into the **Default Behavior Mode** settings, you can change the **Mode**, as shown in the following screenshot:

Selecting 2D mode changes the default settings of Unity for many things. We don't have time to go through all of them in detail, but we can explore the main ones. The scene is always set in 2D with the **Main Camera** in a different position and different settings, such as **Orthographic** mode. Once we have set the asset to the sprite, we have the type of sprite as a second option. By default, it is set to **Single**, but it can be changed to **Multiple** or **Polygonal** (only from Unity 5.3). As the names suggest, the first is used when the imported image contains just a single sprite. The second mode is when we have a sprite sheet with more than one sprite. Finally, the last one is used when we have polygonal sprite, with any number of edges. The **Packing Tag** option is used to gain performance from the graphic card, since Unity merges all the images with the same tag in a unique sheet, which is easier to process for your computer. Therefore, since we don't have any particular need, we can just decide on a name for our **Packing Tag**, and assign it to all our assets. For instance, it could be Badges. Remember that the name must be the same for all our assets in order to include them in the same package. Finally, the last two options that we are going to use are the **Pixel Per Unit** and the **Pivot**. The first is used to tell Unity how big our assets are with respect to our scene. By default, it is set to 100, but this number really depends on how large the images you have imported are. In any case, remember that you can always scale the sprite once it's in the scene. The **Pivot** option, instead, indicates where the pivot points are in the image. It works only if the sprite type is **Single** and it contains a series of presets. Otherwise, by opening the **Sprite Editor**, we can change it into a custom position. Lastly, **Generate Mip Maps** and **Filter** are used for optimization, and we will see them later on.

The Sprite Editor

In the **Import Settings**, you can always find a button labeled **Sprite Editor**. By pressing it, we can open the **Sprite Editor**, as shown in the following screenshot:

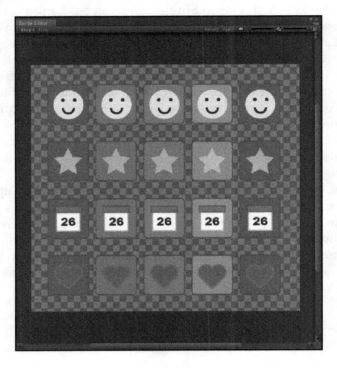

This is a really useful tool in Unity, since it allows us to change the pivot points of Sprites and to identify multiple sprites if we have all of them in a sheet, as in our case. Therefore, its behavior depends on how the **Sprite Type** option is set. In our case, it has to be set to **Multiply** before clicking on the **Sprite Editor**. Unity might ask to apply your changes in **Import Settings** before opening the **Sprite Editor**, and of course we need to accept. There are many ways to use the **Sprite Editor** in Unity, but we don't have the time to go through all of them.

 If you really want to learn every single trick about 2D game development in Unity, and how to use all of these tools, I recommend that you check out the following book: *Getting started with Unity 2D Game Development – Second Edition* by Franscesco Sapio
(www.packtpub.com/game-development/getting-started-unity-2d-game-development-second-edition).

The quickest way possible to select all the sprites is to use **Automatic** mode. In the top left corner of the **Sprite Editor**, there is the **Slice** menu, which we can access by pressing the **Slice** button. For your convenience, it is highlighted in the following screenshot:

The **Slice** menu, once opened, looks like this:

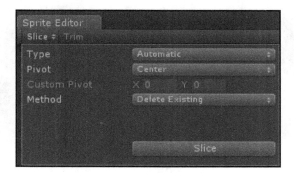

As you can see, we can select different types. However, we will only use the the **Automatic** type. It is the *best guess* of Unity about the selections of the sprites. In fact, there is nothing else to set, Unity will do everything automatically. We don't need to have sprites of the same size; this way works pretty well. Here is the final result applied to our image:

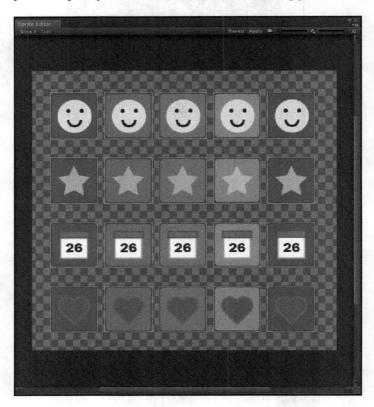

What you may also notice about the preceding screenshot is that each sprite has a box around it, indicating that it has been *sliced* and is ready to go. However, another method to select the sprites in our sheet is just to click and drag a rectangle around the sprite we want. This is the completely **Manual** mode, where you can adjust every single detail. For all the other intermediate ways and tools, refer to the book quoted in the previous info box. Using the manual way, we can select our sprites as follows:

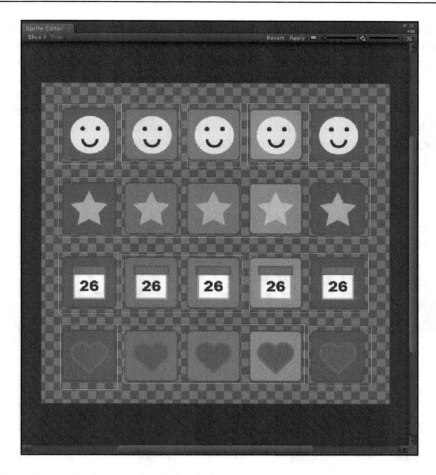

However, just stick with the previous result from the **Automatic** mode, since we don't have any particular need. If you click on one of our selections, it doesn't matter if we created them with the **Automatic** or **Manual** mode, in the bottom right corner we will have the following menu:

This menu also allows us to change the dimension of the selection of the position of its pivot point. These options are for fine tuning, if we really need it. But in this menu, we can also set the name of this specific selection. It is good practice to give a specific name to the selection, especially if the sheet contains different sprites with a different logical meaning. Sprite sheets that have the same meaning are, for instance, animation sheets. In this case, we don't need to rename every single selection, since those sprites are just frames of the same animation. Therefore, if we select the top left selection, we can rename it `SmileBadge_Purple`, as you can see in the following screenshot:

And we can continue renaming all the selections with the same convention. Once we have finished with all the changes in the **Sprite Editor**, click the **Apply** button in the top right corner, as shown in the following screenshot:

If you want to abort your changes and start again, next to the **Apply** button, there is the **Revert** button. As the name suggests, it reverts all the changes. This button is really useful when we get things completely wrong. For your convenience, it is highlighted in the following screenshot:

Testing our settings

Of course, testing that we have selected the **Texture Type** of the Sprites is easy, because otherwise Unity would have allowed us to drag and drop them in the scene. Once you have placed a sprite in the **Scene**, Unity creates a new game object with a **Sprite Renderer** attached, as shown in the following screenshot:

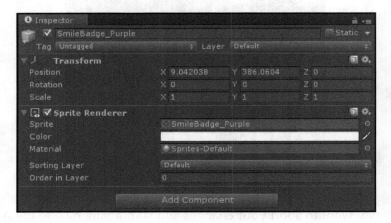

As you can see, the **Sprite** variable is already set with the Sprite we have dragged and dropped.

Testing the packing tag

To see if our assets are included in the right package, we can use the **Sprite Packer**. This tool is available only if the Unity mode is set to 2D. We can access it from the top menu bar by selecting **Window | Sprite Packer**, as shown in the following screenshot:

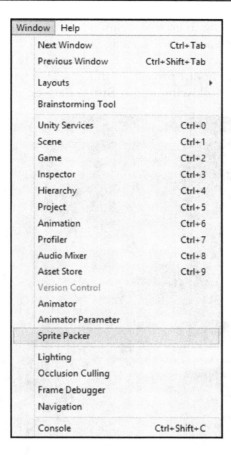

Once opened, this is how it appears:

Unfortunately, we are not going to go into detail about the different policies of packing, but we use this tool just to see the automatic packages or atlases that Unity did when we were setting our packing tags. In fact, from the top bar of the **Sprite Packer**, we can select the different atlases that we have in our project. In this case, we have used the **Badges** tag. Therefore, we should see the following in our **Sprite Packer**:

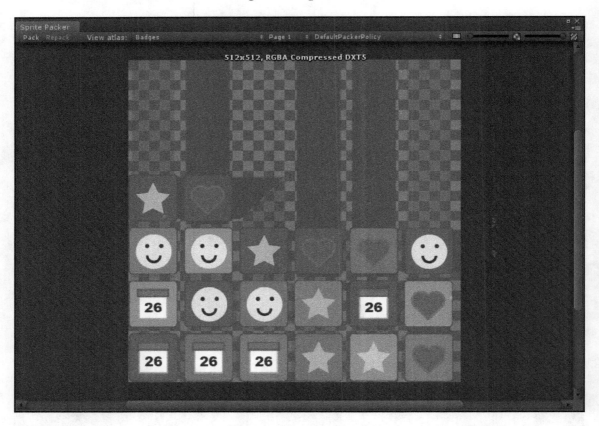

 If you are not able to see your pack, it's because Unity didn't pack it yet. To force Unity to pack, just press the **Pack** button in the top left corner, as highlighted in the following screenshot:

Now, everything looks good. If, for any reason, you want to create another package tag and see how Unity assembles a new atlas in the **Sprite Packer**, feel free to do it. If you want to play with the **Sprite Packer** settings, I suggest that you do it in another project, in order to avoid any inconvenience while we are creating our gamified application here. In fact, the default settings are more than enough for us.

Testing the dimensions of the sprites

As you can imagine, there is not a specific tool for testing the dimensions of the sprites, but, just by using the **Scene** view, we are able to see the dimensions of each Sprite with respect to each other. In fact, this is mainly due the **Pixel Per Unit** option. Now, to test their dimensions, just bring all of them in the **Scene** view, as shown in the following screenshot:

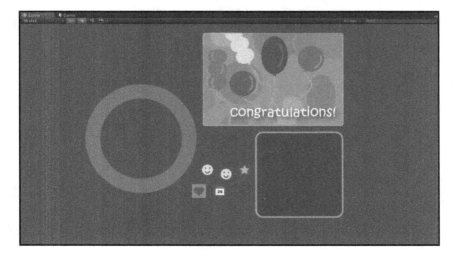

You can just move them around and see if they feel proportional to each other. Of course, what you need to test are the assets into two different sprite sheets. As a result, you can change the **Pixel Per Unit** option to increase (or decrease) their dimensions. The higher the value, the smaller the Sprites will be. In any case, remember that you can always scale single sprites (to be more precise, *the single instances of the sprites in the scene*) as we wish, in order to achieve what we want.

Summary

In this chapter, we started to set everything up for our application. We began with the design of basic assets, which we will need later on. Then, we learned how to use Adobe Illustrator to actually make the assets we need as well as some tips and tricks for using the software. Finally, we moved back into Unity and understood the process of importing assets and made them ready to be used.

In the next chapter, Chapter 7, *Get Your Motor Running*, we will focus on making the most of our application by adding cool new interactive features. Since this is so exciting, don't waste any more time, turn the page!

7
Get Your Motor Running

By now, you should be quite comfortable with using Unity; if not, don't worry, we still have a bit to cover before we are done, and we will be using a lot of what we have already learned. In this chapter, we will implement most of the logic for our application. We will cover the following topics:

- To begin, *Designing our application* will have us designing the UI that will be used in our application.
- Next, *Getting started* will explain how to implement different areas for content within our application, in particular, the lateral menu, the **Home** page, and the **Task** page.
- As we progress through the chapter, *Creating the application interface* will cover how we can create the UI experience.
- In *Defining tasks*, we will learn how to create a custom class in C# that represents the concept of a task in the context of our application, and contains all the information needed in a task.
- Finally, *Dealing with tasks* will explain how to implement a `TaskManager` class that exposes different functions to handle a set of tasks within our application. In addition, it will provide a way to insert a new screen in the application where the user is able to create a new task by choosing different parameters for it.

So, we're going to get our hands dirty, but at the end we will have the application running. As a result, we will be able to focus more on higher-level aspects of our application, such as gamification, in the next chapters. Furthermore, along the way, we will also be developing some skills in the Unity UI and learn how to use it to create the whole application. I didn't say that it will be easy, but for sure it's going to be fun! So, with this said, let's get started.

Designing our application

As we have seen in the previous chapters of this book, the design stage is really important and shouldn't be skipped. This section will give you an overview of what we are going to implement in this chapter.

First of all, we want the user to use a lateral menu to navigate through different parts of the application, as in the following diagram:

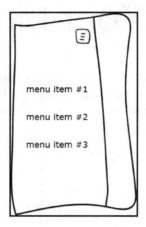

Then, we want to show the tasks to the player, like in the following diagram:

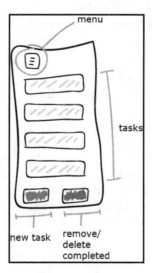

Do you notice the two buttons at the bottom that *create a new task* and *delete completed* ones? We will add this later, but it presents us with some additional functionality to add to the application by creating a new task screen. Of course, we have the profile page, which we created in Chapter 2, *Who or What Am I? Understanding the Player*; following screenshot shows this, just to refresh your memory:

Furthermore, we also have a home page, where for the moment we can just show the profile picture of the user or the logo of the app. Now, with this said, we can start working.

Getting started

In Chapter 6, *Breathing Life into Your First Creation – Creating and Importing Assets for Your Application*, we saw how to create graphics in Illustrator and then how to import them into Unity. However, we didn't take into consideration *all* the graphics that we need to create for the application.

We still need the following graphics:

- A set of icons for our tasks
- A set of icons for our unlockables

- Four icons for the priority of the tasks
- The menu button
- The lateral menu bar
- A background for the different screens of our application

In the following screenshot, we can get an idea of the kinds of graphic that are in the package for this book:

So, I invite you to create your own graphics by revisiting the previous chapter, which covered some basics in Adobe Illustrator. In any case, if you don't have time, or for any other reason you don't want to, you can always download all the graphics for this book from `player26.com`. Again, using your own graphics gives an additional personal touch.

Creating the application interface

Previously, in Chapter 2, *Who or What Am I? Understanding the Player*, we created the profile screen for our application. However, this is only one of application screens that our lateral menu will link to, as shown here:

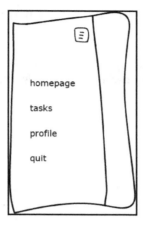

Once we click the menu button, we can then toggle our menu to make it appear or disappear. The following is a list of menu items:

- **Homepage**: Here, the user is able to see the unlocked achievements and their progress
- **Tasks**: This is the main page of our application where the user is able to see all her or his tasks, add new ones, and remove old ones
- **Profile**: This is the page we have already implemented, in which the user is able to change their profile
- **Quit**: This is just a button to close the application

However, we still need to implement a lot of features in our application, since we also need to consider the logic behind it. However, most of these will be covered later in this chapter.

This is an optional step. If you want, you can create a general background for your application, an UI image that is placed on all the screens and has a single color. Moreover, it must be behind everything, so that it doesn't cover the important parts of the application. However, feel free to create a different background for each screen if you prefer.

Now, let's start with the menu, since it is shared among all the screens.

The lateral menu

In this section, we will create our lateral menu. Lateral menus offer an additional type of navigation; many others exist, such as drop-down menus and top navigational bars, which are commonly found on websites. Each different type of menu not only provides a different *feel* for the user, but also some are more suited to an experience than others. For example, if your application is aimed at large screen devices such as tablets, a top navigational bar may be ideal, because there is enough space, and it is unlikely to hinder the experience. On the other hand, having the same type of navigation in a mobile application for a small screen may cause some issues. To solve such problems, it is possible to make the application adapt to the device that it is being experienced on, but this is a topic that we will not cover in this book.

The interface

The first thing to do is to create the button for our menu. To begin, let's create a new image by right-clicking on the **Hierarchy** panel and selecting **UI | Image**. Since this button is always visible, we can leave it parented to the Canvas. In fact, it will just be covered by our lateral menu, since it will contain another button to close it. Now, we can rename it `MenuButton`. Furthermore, in the image component, select the `menu-icon` file from the image pack that we downloaded as a **Source Image**. You should also scale it and place it laterally on the top, as shown in the following screenshot:

Now, click on **Add Component | UI | Button**. Then, change the **Transition** to **None**. In the end, the **Button** component should look like the following:

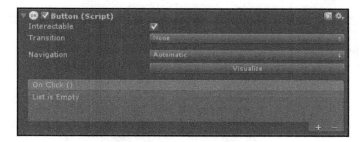

The next step is to create our lateral menu. So, again, create another image by right-clicking on the **Hierarchy** panel and selecting **UI | Image**. Rename the game object `LateralMenu` and use **menu-bar** as the sprite. Finally, place it on the left side of your application, as shown here:

As you can see, the button we have created before is not visible. This is because we want the menu to be on top of everything. If it is not, it is probably because it is not well ordered in the **Hierarchy** panel. Therefore, be sure that the order is like this:

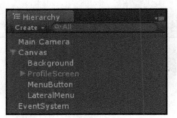

Now, we need to add another menu button, like the previous one, and parent it to **LateralMenu**. We can also duplicate the button we already have by pressing *Ctrl + D* (*cmd + D* on MacOs) and then parent it to **LateralMenu**. The **Hierarchy** panel should be like the following:

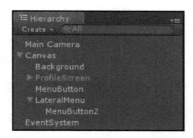

Keep in mind that, when you're duplicating items, the filename will retain the original filename plus the number of the duplicated file. For example, if you're duplicating **MenuButton**, its duplicates will be named **MenuButton (1)**, **MenuButton (2)**, and so on for each duplication. Therefore, you will have to rename them manually to suit your own naming convention.

You need to place this second button at the top of the menu, as shown here:

Opening and closing the menu

Now that we have our two buttons along with the menu, we need to be able to toggle between when the menu opens and when it closes. Let's start by opening the menu.

We need to consider that the menu at the beginning (when the application is lunched) will be disabled. Therefore, opening the menu means enabling it. So, in the first button that we have created, we need to add a new event. To achieve this, click on the small + in the bottom right corner of the **On Click ()** tab. This is how the component appear:

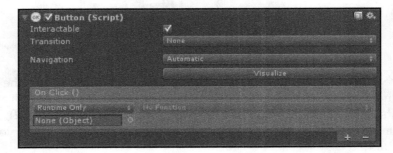

We need to drag and drop **LateralMenu** into the object variable. From the drop-down menu, select **GameObject.SetActive** and check the box below it. This is the final result:

Select the button on the menu and repeat the same steps. However, this time leave the box unchecked, as shown in the following screenshot:

As a result, when we press the first button, the menu appears, and when we press the second button, the menu disappears. Press the **Play** button to test the behavior and check that everything works as it should.

Adding items to the menu

Similar to what we did in the previous section when opening and closing the menu, we do the same with the other screens of our application. When the user selects an option from the menu a screen, all of the other options will be disabled except the one that is selected. This will be enabled instead.

First of all, let's add some UI text. Right-click on **LateralMenu** and select **UI | Text**. Change its color to white and its font style to the one that you defined within your GDD. Furthermore, attach the button component, as before, by pressing **Add Component | UI | Button**. Then, change the **Transition** to **None**. In the end, it should look like the following:

Duplicate this game object as many times as the number of items in our menu, which in this case is four. Rename them, and the Hierarchy panel now should look like the following:

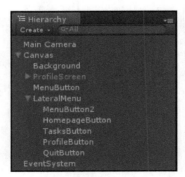

Also, change their text into the items of our menu, and display them on the screen. This is the final result:

Before we can toggle between the other menu screens, we need to create them. We will learn how to do this in the following sections.

The Home page

In this section, we are going to create a game object for our home page. In fact, here we can trigger the homepage. However, we won't implement this in detail, because it's your occasion to test your acquired skills in Gamification. The reason is because this page contains the gamified part of our application. Since the focus of this chapter is on creating the bones of our application to get it running, we won't go in detail on this. In fact, from Chapter 3, *An Engaged Player is a Happy Player*, we are able to implement different game elements, and along what was discussed in all these chapters, you can put them together in a meaningful way, trying to engage your targeting audience. I suggest you to create this part after you have finished this book, so to add some personalization to your application. For now, just create a new UI image that takes up the whole screen, and name it Homepage. As a result, we will have a game object that we can use in this chapter in get all the references to the right places to speed up the process when you will implement this page.

The Tasks page

In this section, we are going to create our Tasks page. However, we will see how to implement all the functionalities with scripting later in this chapter.

First of all, let's create a background image that covers the entire screen. This game object will also be the root for all the other game objects in the screen. Rename it `Tasks Page`. Of course, remember to have this image *before* the menu button and the menu itself in the **Hierarchy** panel. This means they will be visible on the `Tasks Page`.

The main area of the screen will be occupied by tasks. Therefore, we need to create a **Task Displayer**. We can create a UI image and place it in the screen, as shown in the following screenshot:

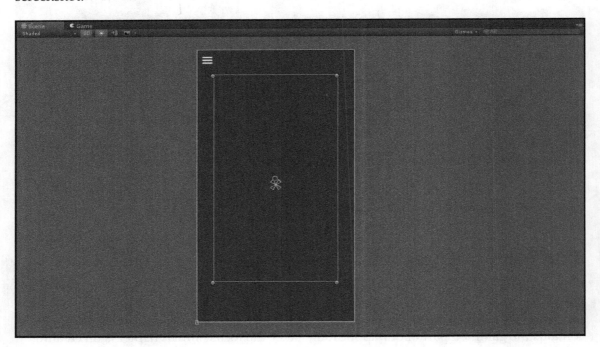

Now that it is placed, we can rename it to `Task Displayer` and remove the image component, since it was only used to place it on the screen. Remember to leave some space at the bottom so that there is room for some buttons that we will add later on.

The basic idea is that the Task Displayer has different **Task Panels**, which contain a specific task. We will see these panels later in the chapter. However, it's important to know how they will be displayed on the screen. Thus, on our Task Displayer, click on **Add Component | Layout | Vertical Layout Group**. Then, disable both checkboxes for **Child Force Expand** and add 19 as **Spacing**. A quick note: if you are having trouble locating the **Padding**, it is likely that the menu is collapsed, so just click on the triangle located next to its name to expand it. At the end, we should have the following:

Of course, feel free to change these settings at the end of the chapter to suit your needs.

At the bottom of the page, in the space that we left before, we need to create two buttons. One is to create a new Task, and the other one is to delete the completed tasks. Therefore, right-click on the **Task Page** in the **Hierarchy** and select **UI | Button**.

In the **Button** component, set **Transition** to **None**. Change the graphics as you prefer and as text insert `New Task`. Duplicate the button with Ctrl + D (Cmd + D on MacOS) and change the text of the second button to `Delete Completed`. Finally, place them as in the following screenshot:

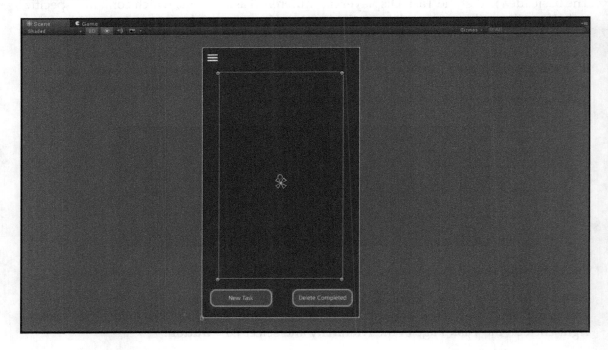

Once we have done all of this, we have finished with the Tasks Page. However, we still need to create an additional page to allow the user to create a new Task. We will implement this after we have defined exactly what a task is in the context of our application.

Navigating through the different screens

Since we have all the different screens, we need to navigate through them. If you remember, we have created different buttons in our lateral menu. Now, we are going to use them.

Let's start from the **Homepage** button in our menu. In the **On Click ()** tab in the **Inspector**, add an event (similar to what we did to open and close the menu). We need to drag the **Homepage** game object into the object variable. From the drop-down menu, select **Game Object | Set Active (bool)** and check the box below. Now, when we click on it, the homepage will be active. However, we need to disable all the other screens, including the later menu.

So, let's add three more events for the remaining screens. Again, drag them in the object variables, and select **Game Object | Set Active (bool)**. This time, don't check the box below, since we have to disable them. This is what it should look like in the **Inspector**:

Similarly, we need to do this for the other buttons by making sure that we enable the correct screen and disable the others. In the end, you should have the following for the **Profile** button:

And you should have the following for the **Tasks** button:

Our menu is now working, with the exception of the **Quit** button, which we still need to implement. However, we will explore this in Chapter 9, *Graduating Your Project to Completion*.

Defining tasks

As we have already mentioned, tasks have a major role in our application. Hence, we need to define what a task is in the context of our application. When we have done this, we will be able to use them like any other class in our scripts, and this will make our life much easier.

Object-oriented

We are programming in C#, which is an object-oriented language. Even though it is not necessary to know exactly how an object-oriented language works to create games in Unity, it is useful. Therefore, I suggest you take a look at any programming book about C# to learn more about the topic.

You should check out one from Packt's library: *C# Programming Cookbook* by *Dirk Strauss*, at `https://www.packtpub.com/application-developmen t/c-programming-cookbook`.

In the next section, we are going to define an **object**. It has different properties and functions that can be called on it.

An example of an object that we are going to use is `DateTime`. It is a class that stores information about a specific date. This is an important and complex object, because you can do a lot of operations on it, such as comparing two dates.

A useful way to imagine these objects is to think them as general and abstract concepts of what we want to represent. Then, they can be an instance and then become that specific object. For instance, we can have the general concept of a horse. This may include the information that it has four legs and one color. Only when we look at a specific horse, can we say that its specific color is brown. However, we need to make sure we represent everything contained in our context or application. For instance, if we include an ordinary horse the information that every horse has four legs is wrong, and must be corrected by including a special case in which the horse has only three legs. In C#, objects are represented by classes. As all the other classes we have used so far, and also Objects are classes. Usually, they don't have any inheritance; for example, when you create a new script in Unity, there is the inheritance of the `MonoBehaviour` class.

The Task class

As usual, we need to create a new script, so right-click on the **Project** panel in the **Script** folder and then select **Create | C# Script**. We can rename it `Task`, because it will represent the concept of a task. First of all, we need to include the system namespace in order to use the `DateTime` class. Then, we need to clean the inheritance from the `MonoBehaviour` class, since we don't need it. As a result, we are not able to attach this script to a game object, but it will contain only what we define inside it. Moreover, delete the `Start()` and `Update()` functions, since this will not be a game object; instead, just a class that we will be able to use in other scripts. At the end, we should have something like the following:

```
using UnityEngine;
using System;

public class Task {

}
```

Now, it's time to add some information about what a Task is. This can be done by including some variables that describe specific aspects of our Task. In particular, we need a string for the title of our Task. We also need a couple of integer variables: one for the priority, since we are going to give them a priority, and another one for the icon, since the user can select one for the task. Finally, we need an expire date, which is the deadline by which the task must to be completed. Therefore, we can write the following:

```
public string title;
public int icon;
public int priority;
public DateTime expireDate;
```

However, we also need a way to check if the Task has already been completed or not. Thus, we can add the following Boolean variable:

```
public bool isCompleted;
```

We have finished describing what a Task is, but we can add some functions to do some operations on them.

First of all, we need a constructor. This is a special function for object-oriented languages, and basically allows us to define some parameters to add when we use the new operator. In this case, we can just set all the variables of our Task. As a result, every time we create a Task, we are sure that all its information is stored. So, we can write the following:

```
public Task(string _title, int _icon, DateTime _expireDate, int
_priority) {
    title = _title;
    icon = _icon;
    expireDate = _expireDate;
    priority = _priority;
}
```

Another operation that we may want on our Task is to check if it has expired. This can be done easily with a function that returns a Boolean value. If it is true, then the task has expired; otherwise, it returns false. So, by using the properties of the DateTime class, we can add the following function:

```
public bool isExpired() {
    if(DateTime.Now > expireDate) {
        return true;
    }
    else {
        return false;
    }
}
```

There is one last function we would like to implement. When we show the task, we also want to know the status of the task. It can be *pending*, if the task is neither completed or expired. If the deadline has passed, it becomes *expired*, and it is *completed* if the user has completed the task. The return value can be a string in order to easily display it. Therefore, we can write the following:

```
public string Status() {
    if (isCompleted) {
        return "Completed";
    } else if(DateTime.Now > expireDate) {
        return "Expired";
    }
    return "Pending";
}
```

At the moment, we don't need to define other functions, but we can always come back to this script and add more. Now that our `Task` class is implemented, save the script. If you open any other script, you are able to use the `Task` class as we were able to use the `DateTime` class, and this is really useful for what we are going to do for the rest of the book.

Dealing with tasks

In this section, we are going to explore how the user can interact with Tasks, how he or she can visualize them, and how to create new ones as well.

A prefab as Task panel

Since the user can create more than one task and we would like to show them in a nice way, we need to create a reusable Task panel. Prefabs are great for reusable objects; therefore, we are going to use one.

First of all, we have to actually create a Task panel in our **Scene** before moving it into a prefab. The general idea is that the Task panel should show all the essential information about a task. This includes the name of the task, its icon, its priority, as well as the expire date. This is the overall design that we would like to achieve:

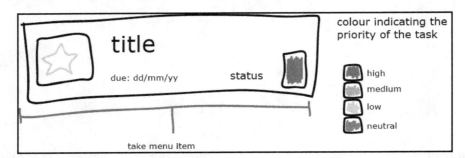

Let's start by creating a new UI image, and use the background in **icons-task** as a sprite. Rename it `Task Panel`. We should have something like the following:

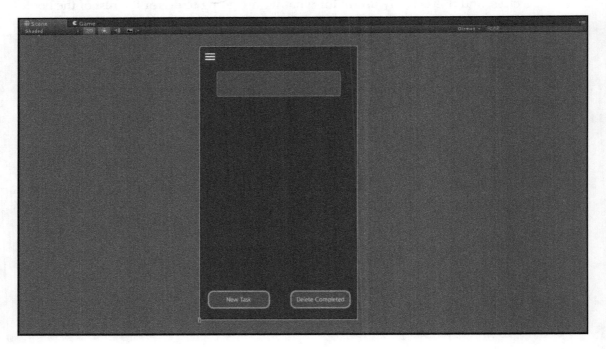

We need to add a new image for the icon on the left, and another one for the priority on the right. Rename the **Icon** and `Priority`. At the moment, you can just leave the default ones by properly scaling them, or use placeholder graphics, as in the following screenshot:

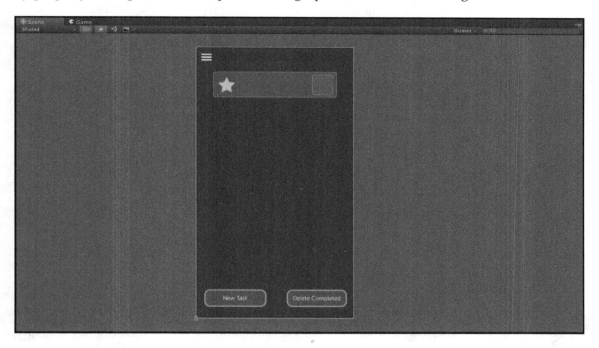

Of course, don't forget to parent them to **TaskPanel**, as shown in the following screenshot:

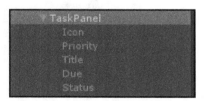

Now, we need to add three text components. One is for the title, one is for the due date, and a third one is for the status. In fact, the status could be *pending*, *expired*, or *completed*. Change the names of the text components to **Title**, **Due**, and **Status**. Don't forget to change them to fit in the visual aspect you have in mind for your application. These changes may include the font and the color, as indicated in the game design document. At the moment, we can use some text placeholders to see how they will look. You need to place them as in the following screenshot:

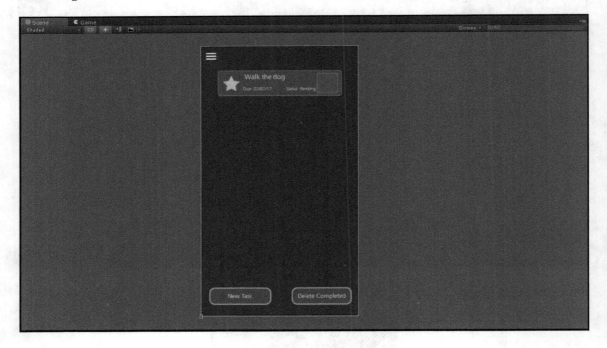

To make it easier to visualize, here is a zoomed-in screenshot to see the placement within the Task panel:

So far so good, but there is still a component missing. The Task panel will be a child of **TaskDiplayer**, which contains a **Vertical Layout Group** component. As a result, it will handle how the Task panel looks. However, we need to tell it how. To achieve this, we can use a **Layout Element** component. Select the **Task Panel**, and click on **Add Component** |

Layout | **Layout Element**. Then, we need to check **Min Width**, **Min Height**, **Preferred Width**, and **Preferred Height**. Based on the dimensions of the Task panel, insert its width and height, repeated for the four variables. In this case, we have a width of 282 and a height of 60. The component should look as follows:

The next step is to create a script that updates all of these components with a task. Therefore, let's create a script. Right-click in the **Project** panel and select **Create** | **C# Script**. You can rename it `TaskPanelScript`. Finally, add it to the **TaskPanel** and double-click on the script to open it. We need to add the UI namespace to use the UI elements in our script. Therefore, let's add the following line at the beginning of the script:

```
using UnityEngine.UI;
```

Furthermore, we can remove both the `Start()` and `Update()` functions, since we don't need them. Then, we need to add a variable for the task that we want to represent, and hide it from the **Inspector**, since we don't need to assign it from there:

```
[HideInInspector]
public Task task;
```

In addition, we need a different variable for all the UI components that we created before in **TaskPanel**:

```
public Image icon;
public Text title;
public Image priority;
public Text status;
public Text due;
```

Since all of the icons and the images for the priority are stored in the Task manager, we need a reference to it as well, and to hide it from the **Inspector**:

```
[HideInInspector]
public TaskManager taskManager;
```

Now we have to create a function that retrieves all the data from the task and shows the task in the Task panel correctly. Therefore, we can write the following:

```
public void UpdateGraphics() {
    title.text = task.title;
    icon.sprite = taskManager.taskIcons[task.icon];
    priority.sprite = taskManager.taskPriorities[task.priority];
    status.text = "Status: " + task.Status();
    due.text = "Due: " + task.expireDate.Date.ToString("dd/MM/yy");
}
```

Plus, we also need a function to mark the task as completed and update the graphics again. So, we can have this:

```
public void taskCompleted() {
    task.isCompleted = true;
    UpdateGraphics();
}
```

Save the script, and come back to the **Inspector**. Attach the script to the **Task Panel** in the **Scene**, and then assign all our variables, as shown in the following screenshot:

Once we have set all of these, we need to give the user the chance to mark this task as completed. Therefore, select the **Task Panel** itself, at the root where the script is attached, and add a button component by clicking on **Add Component** | **UI** | **Button**. As usual, change the **Transition** to **None**. Add a new event in the **On Click ()** tab, and drag the script that we have just created into the object variable. For the function, select **TaskPanelScript.taskCompleted**, as shown in the following screenshot:

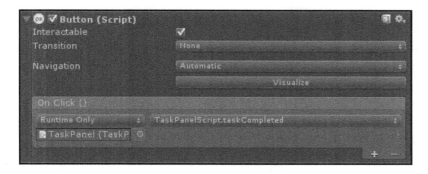

Now, it's time to create a new prefab. Right-click on the **Project** panel and select **Create |**
Prefab. We can rename it `TaskPanelPrefab`. Finally, drag and drop the **TaskPanel** from
our **Scene** inside the prefab. It should now be blue, as shown in the following screenshot:

Now, we are ready to show single tasks, but first we need to handle all of them.

The Task manager

We have defined what a Task is and created a **TaskPanel** to display them; however, there is
nothing that actually handles them. In our application, it's useful to create another script: a
Task manager. As the name suggests, it helps to manage the tasks of the user in the
application. It holds all the tasks of the user, keeps track of which ones are going to expire,
and eventually removes them from the list.

Let's start by creating another script and naming it `TaskManager`. Here, we need to store all
our tasks, and we can achieve it by using an `ArrayList` of tasks:

```
ArrayList tasks = new ArrayList();
```

Then, we need a reference to `taskDisplayer` as well as a reference to the prefab of the **TaskPanel**:

```
public GameObject taskDisplayer;
public GameObject taskPanelPrefab;
```

These last two variables must be set in the **Inspector** in order to make our script work. Then, since `TaskManager` is the central hub for handling tasks, we need to also store the icons for the tasks as well as the images for the priority. So, let's add a couple of sprite arrays for them:

```
public Sprite[] taskIcons;
public Sprite[] taskPriorities;
```

Now that we have defined our data, let's create a useful function to manipulate them. We can have a function that removes all completed tasks:

```
public void deleteCompleted() {
    for (int i = tasks.Count - 1; i >= 0; i--) {
        if (((Task)tasks[i]).isCompleted)
            tasks.RemoveAt(i);
    }

    OnEnable();
}
```

This function basically iterates in the `ArrayList` of Tasks and checks if they are completed. In this case, the function removes them from the array. First of all, you can see that the `for` loop is going backwards. The reason for this is that, when we remove from an array going backwards, it doesn't mess with the indexes while the script is looping on it. Second, at the end, we call the `OnEnable()` function, which basically resets the graphics. We are going to implement this function right now.

 As an exercise, you can implement a function to remove expired tasks and update the graphics in a similar way. The logic is the same as before, the difference being that it checks for expired tasks rather than completed ones.

Every time `TaskManager` is enabled, it has to update the graphics. We can do this by implementing the `OnEnable()` function. Here, we need to remove all the previous **TaskPanels** and create new ones parented to `taskDisplayer`. So, we can write the following:

```
void OnEnable() {
    //Destroy all the previous tasks
    for (int i = 0; i < taskDisplayer.transform.childCount; i++) {
        Destroy(taskDisplayer.transform.GetChild(i).gameObject);
    }
    if (tasks.Count > 0) {
        //Create a new task panel for each of them
        foreach (Task t in tasks) {
            GameObject temp = Instantiate(taskPanelPrefab);
            temp.transform.SetParent(taskDisplayer.transform);
            temp.GetComponent<TaskPanelScript>().task = t;
            temp.GetComponent<TaskPanelScript>().taskManager = this;
            temp.GetComponent<TaskPanelScript>().UpdateGraphics();
        }
    }
}
```

We have one more operation to implement! We need to provide the possibility of adding a new task to the tasks list. This can be done easily in the following way:

```
public void addTask(Task t) {
    tasks.Add(t);
}
```

Finally, we have completed the `TaskManager`. If you have followed this all through from start to finish, I now encourage you to take a break, and enjoy a nice beverage or something to eat, because you've earned it! In the next section, we will see how to allow the user to create new tasks.

Allowing the user to create new Tasks

Now we have to create another page to allow the user to create a new task. As usual, it is a background image that is the root of our page. However, this time, the page should be on top of the lateral menu and its button. This is because we don't want the user to change the page while he or she is creating a task. At this stage, you should have acquired a good knowledge of the UI of Unity; therefore, this section explains what we need to do, but not step by step, as before. In fact, most of the steps needed are the same as when we created a button or an image.

Create Task button

Near the bottom of the screen, place a button with the label `Create Task`. When the user clicks on this button, a new task will be created. As a result, the `TaskManager` list will be updated as well. It should be placed as in the following screenshot:

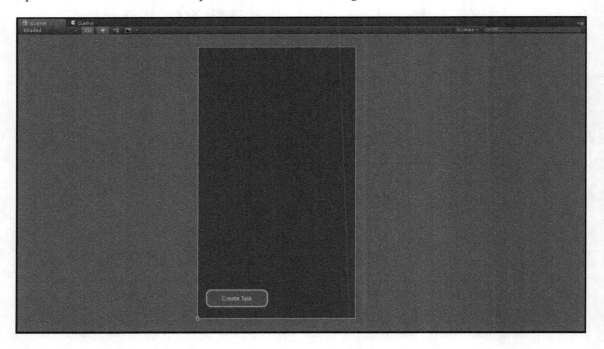

We need to create a new script in which the different variables will be set by the components we are going to create in the upcoming sections. Name the script `CreateTask` and open it.

To begin, we need to create four private variables, one for each aspect of a task:

```
private int priority;
private string title;
private string due;
private int icon;
```

Since they are `private`, we need to create some functions to let the other components of the page update them:

```
public void setPriority(int p) {
    priority = p;
}

public void setIcon(int i) {
    icon = i;
}

public void setDue(string d) {
    due = d;
}

public void setTitle(string t) {
    title = t;
}
```

Now, we also need a public variable, so set it in the **Inspector**, to store the `TaskManager`:

```
public TaskManager taskManager;
```

Finally, we need the function that will be called when the button is pressed. First, there is a series of checks (left as an exercise) to see if the data inserted by the user is valid. Then, a new task is created by using the data stored in the variables. In fact, these variables will be set while the user is inserting the data in the page to create the task. Therefore, we can write the following:

```
public void Create() {
    //CHECKS!
    DateTime date = DateTime.ParseExact(due, "dd/MM/yy",
CultureInfo.InvariantCulture);
    taskManager.addTask(new Task(title, icon, date, priority));
}
```

Save the script and attach it to the button. Don't forget to drag and drop `TaskManager` into the right variable as well.

Now, in the **On Click ()** event tab, we need to add an event to trigger the last function we wrote in the script. Then, we need another couple of events to close the **Create Task Page** and open the **Tasks Page** again. This is the final result:

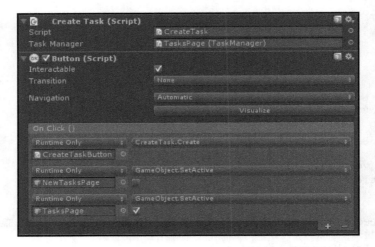

Delete task button

What happens if the user doesn't want to create the task anymore? In this situation, we need to add a second button with the label **Cancel**. In the **On Click ()** event tab, just close the **New Task Page** and open the **Tasks Page**, as shown in the following screenshot:

The button should be placed here, next to **Create Task**:

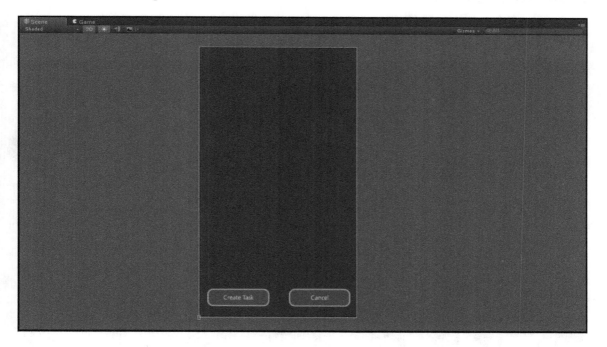

Adding the icon

At the top of the page, we need to add a text label and an image, as shown in the following screenshot:

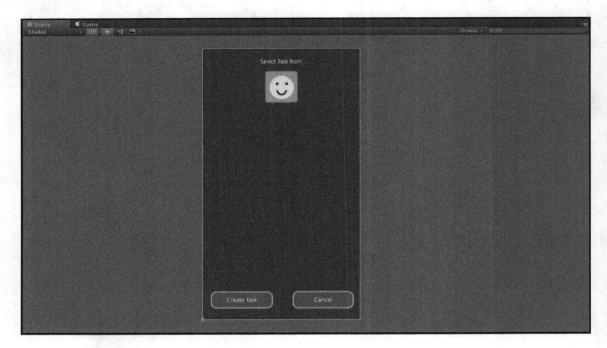

When the user clicks on the image, it changes, allowing the user to see the different options. Therefore, we need to add the button component to the image (**Add Component** | **UI** | **Button**) and set the **Transition** to **None**.

Create a script named SelectTaskIcon and attach it to the image. Since we are going to use the UI image class, we need to add the following line at the beginning of our script:

```
using UnityEngine.UI;
```

In the script, we have two public variables to store `TaskManager` and `CreateTask`, and a private variable for a counter:

```
public TaskManager taskManager;
public CreateTask createTask;
private int counter;
```

Then, we need to create a function that's called when the image is clicked. The counter is updated, the icon on the image is shifted, and the change is communicated to `CreateTask`. Please notice that the icons are taken from `TaskManager`:

```
public void OnClick() {
    counter++;
    if (counter == taskManager.taskIcons.Length)
        counter = 0;
    GetComponent<Image>().sprite = taskManager.taskIcons[counter];
    createTask.setIcon(counter);
}
```

Save the script and set the two public variables in order to have the reference to `TaskManager` and `CreateTask`. Then, add a new event in the button component. Drag the script that we have just created into the object variable and select the function we created in the script from the drop-down menu, as shown in the following screenshot:

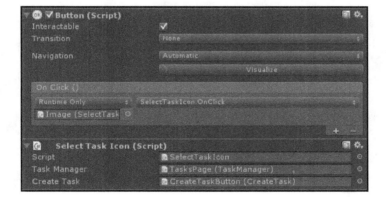

Inserting the title

Let's create a label, as before, and an input field where the user can insert the name of the task. Now, create a new event in the **End Edit (String)** tab, and drag `CreateTask`. Select, in the dynamic parameters, the **setTitle()** function, as shown in the following screenshot:

The final result in the **Scene** view is shown here:

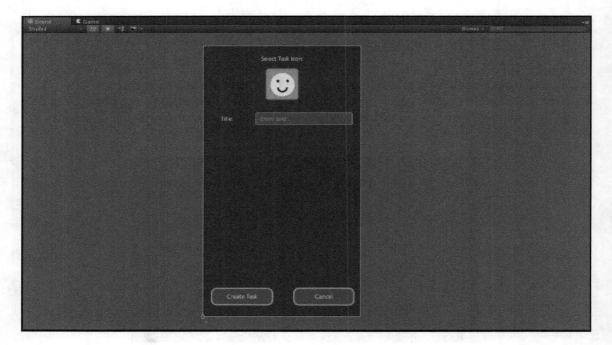

Inserting the Due date

Similar to the previous section, we need to create a label and an input field where the user can insert the due date of the task. Then, we need to create a new event in the **End Edit (String)** tab, then drag the `CreateTask` into it. Set the dynamic parameters in the **setDue()** function, as shown in the following screenshot:

As a result, it should appear like the following in the **Scene** view:

Selecting the Task priority

For the task priority, we need to create four images, one for each priority: **Neutral** (green), **Low** (yellow), **Medium** (orange), and **High** (red). So, once we have used the sprite we want (you can choose the ones in the packages, or use one that you created in the previous chapter), we should place them as the following screenshot shows:

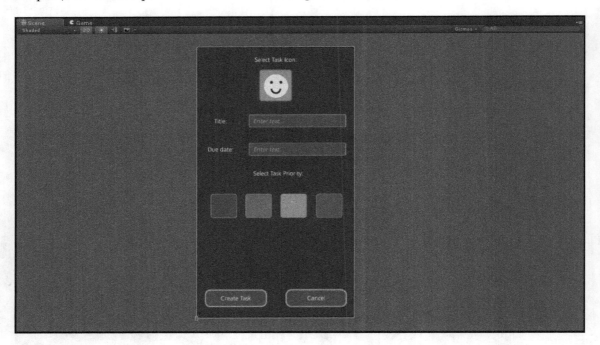

Add the button component to all of them, and set the **Transition** to **None**. Add a new event in the **On Click ()** tab and drag `CreateTask` into the object variable. Finally, select **setPriority()** as a function. However, we need to change the value for each priority. We have the value 0 for neutral, 1 for low, 2 for medium, and 3 for high.

If you want to, you can add another label to give some visual feedback to the user about the priority he or she has selected. In this case, you need to add another event to all the priorities and insert the label into the object variable. Then, select the text that the label will contain as a function and change the value for each priority. In the end, you should have all the event tabs set as follows, which, for the sake of simplicity, are combined into a single screenshot:

By doing this, we have finished with the **Create a New Task** page. Remember to save your file and take a break, because more exiting tasks await!

Setting up the Tasks page

Because you have already implemented the Task panel and the Task manager, it is simple to finish the Tasks page. First of all, attach the Task manager script to the page itself, if you didn't before. In fact, we have already placed a reference to it in the previous scripts. Therefore, before continuing, check if they are correct. Then, we need to assign its variables, such as the reference to `TaskDisplayer` and the prefab of the Task panel. Furthermore, remember to also assign icons in these variables that the user can select as icons for his or her tasks, and the priority. We should have something like the following screenshot:

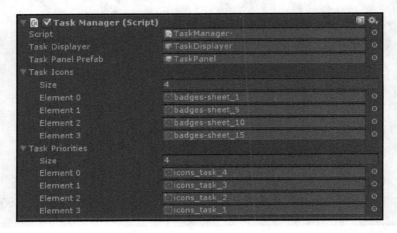

Now it's time to add some functionality to the two buttons on the page. In **Create Task**, we just need to close the Tasks page and open the **Create Task Page**, as shown in the following screenshot:

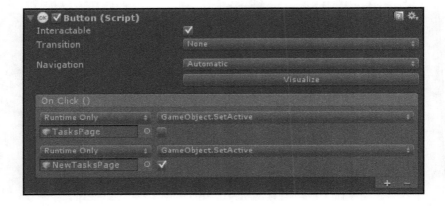

For the other button, we just need to call the function on the Task manager in order to delete all of the completed tasks, as in the following screenshot:

Finally, save the scene, and we should now have the entire task system working in our application.

Summary

In this chapter, we have implemented most of our application. In fact, all the main logic has been implemented. The user is now able to visualize the tasks in a nice and ordered way. Furthermore, he or she is able to mark them as completed and eventually remove them. Plus, the user can create new tasks with a form. In addition, he or she can navigate through the application with a lateral menu. I'd say that, so far, we have achieved a lot! However, our application is not finished, because we still need to refine it. In saying that, now it is time to get ready to immerse yourself in the next chapter, where we will learn how to playtest our creation!

8
Break, Destroy, and Rebuild - the Art of Playtesting and Iteration

In this chapter, the reader will learn about methods of playtesting and iteration in order to improve their design. We will suggest ways to test, what to look for, and what to pay attention to during this stage. We will learn about these and a few other things along the way in the following sections:

- To begin, *Playtesting* will describe the basics of developing your playtest, from types of playtesting to who you need to test your application.
- Next, *Methods of play testing – game time* will explain how to go about your playtest and various things that need to be taken into account both before and after you have finished testing.
- Now that our application has reached the final stages, *After the game* will cover what to do once you have finished playtesting and how to use the information as part of the iterative process.
- After reflecting on the feedback from playtesting, *Iteration* will explain the iteration process and the main cycle used in this book to iterate.
- Before concluding this chapter, *Data persistence in our application* covers the concept of data persistence and different ways to achieve it in Unity. As a result, the application won't restart from scratch at every launch.
- Lastly, *Connecting the application to a database* will explain how to connect Unity to a database for persistent data storage in order to collect data easier for playtesting and further analysis.

Playtesting

This is one of the most important parts of your game design. In fact, you cannot expect to have a great game without it. Playtesting is not just about seeing if your game works, or if there are bugs; it is also about finding out what people really think about it before you put it out there for the world to see. In some cases, playtesting can be the difference between succeeding or failing epically. Consider this scenario: you have spent the last year, blood, sweat, and tears, even your soul, creating something fantastic. You probably think it's the best thing out there. Then, after you release it, you realize that only half the game was balanced, or worse, half interesting. At this stage, you are going to feel pretty down, but all this could have been avoided if you had taken the time to get some feedback. As humans, we don't necessarily like to hear our greatest loves being criticized, especially if we have committed so much of our lives to it. But the thing to keep in mind is that this stage shapes the final details.

Playtesting is not meant for the final stages, when your game is close to being finished. At each stage, even once you begin to get a basic prototype completed, it should be playtested. During these stages, it does not have to be large-scale testing; it can be a few colleagues, friends, or even family giving you an idea of whether or not you're heading in the right direction. The main thing here is to really stress that you need honest feedback, even if it's perhaps not something you want to hear. Of course, the other important thing to keep in mind is that the people who are testing your game are as close as possible to, if not *the*, target audience. For instance, imagine that you're creating a gamified application to encourage people to take medication on a regular basis. It is not ideal to test it with people who do not take medication. Sure, they may be able to give general feedback, such as UI elements or even interaction, but in terms of its effectiveness, you're better off taking the time to recruit more specific people.

Methods of playtesting

There are many different ways to approach the playtesting phase. There is no right or wrong way to go about it. However, there are some things that need to be considered and included during the playtesting phase. Playtesting can be done by oneself, and it can also be done with others. Ideally, having people who are from your target audience is the preferred place to start. However, we will also look at how to get valuable information, when your playtesters aren't from your target group.

Going solo

This might seem like an obvious thing, but even if you think you have developed the Holy Grail of playtesting criteria, it is more than likely you've forgotten something. This is why it is important that you playtest with yourself or your team. It is even worthwhile to playtest with a small group of others before rolling out a larger-scale playtesting session. Not only does this show you how you want to test the application, it will also help you to shape and focus your questions about their experience, whether it is a verbal discussion or a survey.

Group testing

The more the merrier, and it's the same with is playtesting. When you have group testing, it is important to not only have people from your target demographic, but other people as well. This is because they may be able to offer valuable feedback from a different perspective.

Open or controlled

This is the same question as asking whether your playtest is going to be public or private. Do players need to sign a non-disclosure agreement, or can they freely and openly talk about the game to anyone after they have played? This is a very important consideration, because if you want to keep the contents of your game private until release, you don't want people posting about it on Facebook. Other considerations can be asking playtesters not to take any videos or pictures during testing. In some cases, especially for online games, the **Print Screen** option is disabled. While there are many workarounds to this, by getting participants to adhere to a set of rules prior to playtesting (for example, signing an agreement), you can avoid any unwanted publicity later.

Getting the info – have a plan!

Testing is fine, but without an objective, it is redundant. Ask yourself questions such as: What am I hoping to get from playtesting my game or application? Am I trying to find out if a particular part of the application works in a certain way, or if the application is interesting as a whole? Playtesting can be as simple as focusing on one of these things, or as complex as focusing on all of them. Of course, the latter would require different approaches, and even segmenting your playtesting group to focus on each element. Ideally, though, you want to make sure that important features are tested, not trivial ones.

Recruiting the chosen ones!

So now, you have *how* you're going to playtest; the next step is to find *who*. These people can range from those that you know, don't know, people within physical proximity (for example, testing in a physical location), or virtual testing (for example, testing over a distance using downloads). The other thing to keep in mind is who you want playing your game and whether or not they will be the ones who *do* play your game in the end. Getting feedback from a group of school children for an application that is aimed at finance management is not going to give you the insights or data that you're looking for. While in some cases you might be limited to who you can get to test your game, try to get testers within your demographic. If you can't, then it's about asking the questions that will give you valuable information to improve the application for those who will play it.

People you know

You can always start with your friends, family, and other close associates if you want to get some quick feedback about a particular part of your application, or even as a second pair of eyes along the way.

People you don't know

Sometimes, it's great to get comments from those that we know. This is because we feel comfortable with them, and in some instances they tell us what we want to hear, which is counterintuitive.

Once you get some basic feedback from those that you know, get the opinion of those you don't.

The people who you are targeting

Given all this talk about people, it is important to keep in mind *who* you are intending your game or application to be for. Perhaps this is in the very early stages and you're still trying to figure out if it's for a specific age range or for everyone. In any event, put together a *user profile* of the kinds of attribute that they may have. This will also help you to improve the design for your playtest. In this way, you are able to focus questions that are related to the relevance of the application to them and find out (if necessary) what could make it more relevant.

Setting up the play-date for playtesting

Now that you have decided *who* will be a part of your playtest, you still need to figure out *where, when,* and *how*. Then you need to ask yourself some basic questions, such as Do I need a large space to playtest in? Can playtesters bring their own devices, or will you supply them with one?

A little goes a long way

Will you be compensating your playtesters in any way? One thing to consider if you have limited funds is buying some snacks or drinks to supply them with during testing. If it is a long time, if they are giving up their time to help you out, it is nice to give something back to say thank you.

Getting everyone on the same page

You will need to get everyone up-to-speed, and the best way to do this is to give a brief introduction to what you will be doing. You can do this in any number of ways, such as a small presentation or even a handout explaining the game/application and the purpose of the playtesting. It doesn't matter which way you do it, as long as it brings everyone up-to-date about the point of them coming.

Play time!

Now that everyone knows the details of what they are required to do, it's time to actually do it. There is no particular strategy to get users testing. For example, you may want users to play within the same room, isolated, with or without headphones, and so forth. These factors are entirely up to you because, ideally, it comes back to what kind of information you are looking to gain. If one element that you're focusing on is the audio effects during gameplay, then it would be better for participants to use headphones. Perhaps it is a social game in which you want players to interact with each other; in this case, the space should be designed to facilitate that. Do you need tables, chairs, perhaps have some music in the background to break the formality and create a relaxed atmosphere? These are some important things to keep in mind when you're choosing and designing the space for playtesting. It can also be things like this that affect a playtester's mood as well. Being kept in a small room, with no open windows for a couple of hours with 12 other people may not be the most pleasant experience; they will probably want to finish quickly and leave.

Another thing to keep in mind is the duration of the playtest. For example, you may need an application to be tested over a 5, 10, or even 30-day period to really determine if it achieves what you want it to, or at least part of it. Therefore, you need to consider if, in these instances, playtesters need to come to a specific place to engage (if so, are you able to compensate them?) or they are able to playtest from the comfort of their home.

Methods of playtesting – game time!

Why are players playing your application? Ask them questions such as *Why did you do that?*, *Do you understand the rules or is it confusing?*, or *Did you expect that to happen?*. Getting feedback at these crucial moments can let you know whether the game is being played and understood as it should be. Of course, you need to keep in mind what you want information about, as the preceding questions are very general. This is a good place to begin, but as the testing develops you will want to ask more specific questions, such as *Did you feel more motivated when you received a badge?* or *Is it tedious having to select from a large array of options?*.

Observing how testers are playing

While testers are interacting with your game, observe *how* they are doing it, just like in the following screenshot. Do they engage in a particular way that is not intended? This may demonstrate that you have some glitches in your experience that could even be exploited. For example, if players are able to find ways around certain elements to get more points, obtain badges, and so forth, you will need to revise. The same can be said for the reverse, if players are supposed to obtain something but they don't, or the game won't allow them to progress. At these points, players may find the game boring because of a technical issue.

Asking the right questions

When you begin playtesting, you should have in mind what you want to achieve. This will also help you to focus your questions, whether it is in a survey or in an interview. The importance of this is that you don't want to have too much general information if you are testing a particular part of your game or application.

During the playtest

Depending on how long you will have playtesters engaged with your game, it may be ideal to take breaks. This is also a good opportunity to get some feedback along the way. For example, perhaps there is a particular part of the game that they are experiencing at that moment that could be important for you to know. This is your chance to gain some insight into what they are experiencing so far and for you to gauge the *initial* impressions. During this time, it is likely that your potential users will make the decision to either keep using your game or uninstall it. So, if some playtesters are leaning more towards the latter, find out why.

After the game

Asking playtesters directly about their experience with your game or application will give you a lot more detailed information about why certain elements were good, and others will not give you so much. For example, one tester may like the Leaderboards because it gave them a sense of achievement, and the other may like them because they enjoyed being better than everyone else. These two varying opinions are useful; if your intention was to encourage competition, then at least you know that to some extent, it's working.

Asking them to explain the game to you

"If you can't explain it simply, you don't understand it well enough."
— Albert Einstein

The same can be said about your game. If players can't describe what your game is about, or what it is supposed to achieve in its simplest form, then it's not clear enough. This could be because the rules are ill-defined or that the objectives are not clear enough. Perhaps your intention was to create a role-playing application to encourage students to submit their homework on time, but playtesters say that it's a *time-management application*. While some of that might be true, it's not your intended idea. From here, you can begin to understand why.

Keeping it balanced with rules

Another thing to consider is asking playtesters about the rules. Were the rules clear enough? Were they fair? Could they be improved? These types of question can also help to balance your game. If higher-level players have significant advantages over lower-level players, then it may be too difficult for them to engage with one another, whether it is to work together or against each other. Another important question to ask is weather any glitches occurred. While your rules may have been understandable, there may still be opportunities for players to gain an advantage. If so, it's better to fix it now than to find out after you have published it from some unhappy players.

Interacting and the interface

So the game may be balanced, super fun to play, but the interface is ruining it for everyone. Perhaps you have a beautiful interface, but the gameplay just isn't fun. Well, find out why! Do players have difficulty with the controls of the application. For example, they swipe left and it goes right, or the button *sometimes doesn't work*. Maybe that big red close button is just a little too big *or red*. Things like this can really ruin an experience. For example, it can be extremely frustrating when you keep hitting *next* to select something and nothing happens; and then all of sudden you're going at the speed of light through all the choices. If it happens once, some players can be forgiving, but if it is a constant issue, they will be heading for the uninstall option.

Post-mortem – evaluating the playtest

So, what did everyone think? This is where you get some general feedback about what the playtesters experienced. After this point, you can begin to refine the discussion. They may all like the intro sequence, but why? Maybe one of them thought the music was great, and the others liked the visuals.

Reflecting at the end of it all

By now, the playtesters have gone home. You're left with an empty testing space and a whole bunch of notes, ideas, and different thoughts that are going through your mind. Now is the time to get them down, on paper, in a Word document, wherever, but write them down! This is where you think about what is going right and wrong in your game, whether it was part of an intended feature or not. This is an important process because what happens here can greatly impact your game upon release.

 If you want to read more about playtesting, you should check out the following book: *Game Design Workshop: A Playcentric Approach to Creating Innovative Games* by *Tracy Fullerton*.

Iteration

After we have done all the playtesting, is time to plan another development cycle. In fact, the work of tuning your application doesn't stop after the first tests. On the contrary, it goes through different iterations many times.

The iteration cycle

The cycle starts with the planning stage, which includes brainstorming, organizing the work (as we have seen, for instance, in Scrum), and so on. In the next phase, development, we actually create the application, as we did in the last chapter. Then, there is the playtesting, which we have seen in this chapter. In the latter stage, we tune and tweak values, as well as fix bugs in our application.

Afterwards, we iterate the whole cycle again, by entering the planning stage again. Here, we need to plan the next iteration, what should be left, what should be done better, and what to remove. All these decisions should be based on what we have collected in the playtesting stage. The cycle is well represented in the following figure as a spiral that goes on and on throughout the process:

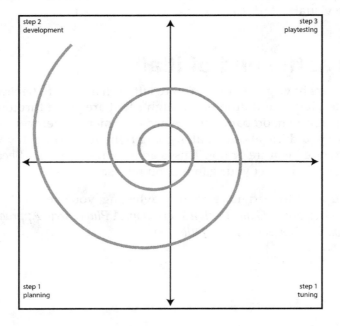

The point of mentioning it now is because, after you have finished playtesting your game, you will need to repeat the stages that we have done previously. You will have to *modify* your design, you may need to even redesign things. So, it is better to think of this as *upgrading* your design, rather than a tedious and repetitive process.

When to stop?

In theory, there is no stopping. The more iteration there is, the better the application will be. Usually, the iterations stop when the application is good enough for your standards, or when external constraints, such as the market or deadlines, don't allow you to perform any more iterations.

The question *when to stop?* is tricky, and the answer depends on many factors. You need to take into account the resources needed to perform another iteration, as well as time constraints. Of course, remember that your final goal is to deliver a quality product to your audience, and each iteration is a step closer.

Data persistence in our application

In the previous chapter, we implemented most of the logic of our application. However, every time the user closes the application, all their tasks disappear. This is because our application is not persisting data.

To make data persistent, we need in some way to store it. The first intuitive way is to store the data locally, which means saving to a file.

PlayerPrefs in Unity

Unity offers a quick and easy way to store data persistently by using `PlayerPrefs`, a special class where there are functions to save primitives, such as integers or strings. In the following examples, we will work with strings, but the process is the same for all the other primitives.

The Set function

It is possible to save the data by using the following line:

```
PlayerPrefs.SetString("Your Key", "Your Value");
```

Basically, it takes a key and a value. The key is important, because we need it when we need to get the value back, maybe in another session (the user used the application, closed it, and re-opened it).

Therefore, in our case, we need to save every task when the user performs any operation, such as creating a new one or deleting some. The implementation of this is left as an exercise.

Tasks, like classes, are not primitives. Therefore, you need to create a function that uses `PlayerPrefs` several times to store just one task by using iterative keys. In addition, you can use this function to save all the tasks from `TaskManager`.

Remember to also store the number of tasks, so your function knows how many tasks with iterative keys it needs to retrieve.

The Get function

The sister of the previous function is the `Get` function. You can retrieve the value of `PlayerPrefs` by using his key as a parameter of the following function:

```
PlayerPrefs.GetString("Your Key");
```

As a result, you get the value, so be sure to store it in a variable. In addition, if the value doesn't exist (there is no value associated with that specific key), you can set a default values with the following line:

```
PlayerPrefs.GetString("Your Key", "Default value");
```

As before, we need to use the same key we have used when we called the `set` function.

In our case, once the user opens the application, all the tasks should be loaded. This can be done by using the get function. Again, the implementation is left as an exercise.

Like before, you can create a function that uses different `PlayerPrefs` to get functions to retrieve a task, and create a new task with those features. Then, another function can use the previous to load all the tasks in `TaskManager`. Eventually, don't forget to update the graphics too.

Erasing an entry

To erase an entry from `PlayerPrefs`, we need its key, and then we call the following function:

```
PlayerPrefs.DeleteKey("Your Key");
```

As a result, the value of that key is erased. This might be helpful if we want to clean the extra tasks we stored in the previous section, if the user has erased some of them.

Erasing all the data

If, for any reason, we want to delete all the data, we can just use the following line:

```
PlayerPrefs.DeleteAll();
```

> Be careful, since this operation is irreversible. Pay attention to where you place this line in your code.

Saving local data in a custom file

If we are not a fan of `PlayerPrefs`, a more flexible way is to create a file on our own.

We can actually encrypt it and decrypt if we wish, and store it where we want. However, doing this includes dealing with streams. They are an advanced topic in programming, and we don't have time to go through them here. Therefore, I suggest you read any book about C# I/O (input/output) operations.

Using a database

The last way to have persistent data is to store it in a database. This approach has its own advantages and disadvantages. The main pros are as follows:

- Device-independent
- Flexible
- Data synchronization
- Multiple users
- Easier analysis of the data

On the other hand, the cons are as follows:

- Requires an Internet connection
- Might be slow and very difficult to implement

However, in the next section, we will see a simple solution to connect a database to our application.

Connecting our application to a database

In this section, we will explore the different options we have to connect our application to a database. Of course, we are going to see numerous options, but, for sure, this is a good start, especially for those who have never connected an application to a database before.

Why are databases important for playtesting?

First of all, we need to understand why databases are important for playtesting. As we have seen in the previous sections, playtesting is mainly about collecting data from the players/users and using this data to improve our game. However, this data must to be stored somewhere, and that's why a database becomes handy.

In fact, we can store data locally, but this would limit the playtesting to only being in-studio, whereas having a database where our application can send data allows us to distribute beta or alpha versions among playtesters.

Services for databases

Once we have decided to use a database for our application, we have two options: we develop a database on our own, or we use a service. Of course, the first solution is much more flexible, but it takes time, resources, and an entire other book to explain. For this reason, we will use an existing service. There are many different services for Unity, but for the project in this book, we are going to use a service called Playfab.

Playfab in Unity

Playfab is a *backend platform for games*. In fact, you can also handle more complex interactions rather than just being limited to storing and getting data. For instance, a user can register and get specific data, or analytics, that can be computed on your database.

Another great thing is that Playfab is free. There are some paid plans that offer more features. However, for the sake of this book, the free plan is more than enough. You can download it from their site, `https://playfab.com/`:

Downloading the SDK from the website

Playfab is not limited to Unity, but also works with other different platforms or development environment. Therefore, the first thing to do is to download the SDK from the website. You can download it from the following link:

`https://playfab.com/unity-sdk-v2-released/`

You need to click on **SDK Here**. For your convenience, it is highlighted in the following screenshot:

Importing and setting the SDK in Unity for databases

Be sure to have your project opened in Unity, and double-click on the file you have downloaded. Once you have done that, you should see the following import screen:

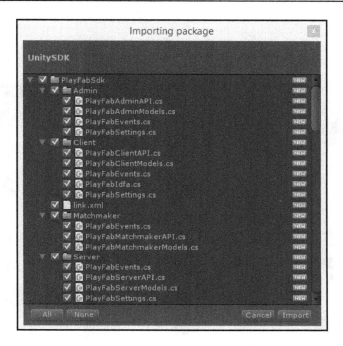

Click on **Import**, and wait for Unity to import everything. At the end, the package has added two additional folders, as shown in the following screenshot. One is called **PlayFabSdk**, and the other one **Plugins**:

The **Plugins** folder is a special folder in Unity, so you might already have it in the project. In any case, don't ever rename that folder or move the files within it. In fact, if you do, Unity is not able to detect the Playfab plugin anymore.

The next step is to register for a Playfab account. You can do it from this link:

```
https://developer.playfab.com/en-us/sign-up
```

The whole process is pretty straightforward: all you need to do is provide your e-mail address, along with the password, twice, and accept the terms and conditions. Then, click on **CREATE A FREE ACCOUNT**:

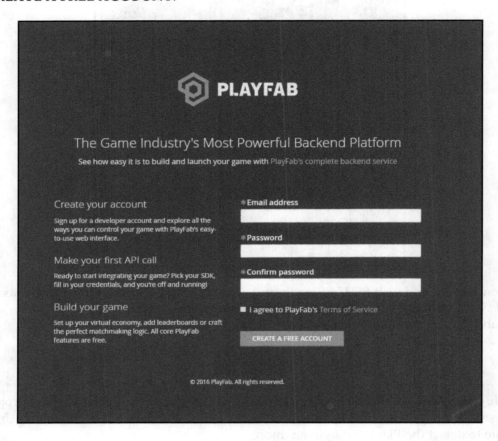

Afterwards, Playfab gives you **Unnamed Studio** with an **Unnamed Title** as defaults. Feel free to change these to more meaningful names that suit your project:

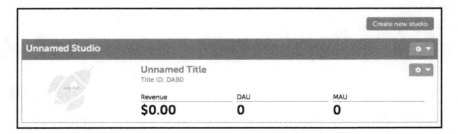

Furthermore, by clicking on the cog in the top right corner, you have access to the contextual menu.

Creating a login system for your users

Now, that is everything set up, let's see how to create a login system using Playfab.

First, let's create a new C# script and name it `LoginWithPlayfab`. Then, double-click to open it. Every time we use Playfab, we need to specify this in our script by using the corresponding `using` statements. In our case, we need to add these two at the beginning of our script:

```
using PlayFab;
using PlayFab.ClientModels;
```

Then, we need to initialize Playfab in the `Start()` function, by writing the following code:

```
void Start () {
    PlayFabSettings.TitleId = "YOUR TITLE ID";
}
```

 Of course, instead of YOUR TITLE ID, insert yours. A quick note about YOUR TITLE ID: the ID will have been created when you registered your account.

Now, we need a variable to store the ID for the API calls after the login, so we can have the following code:

```
public string PlayFabId;
```

Finally, we can write a function for the login, which takes the title id as a parameter. Here, we can write two functions/statements. The first one needs to create a data structure to send to the server, and the other one asks the server to log in. To make the data structure, we use `LoginWithCustomIDRequest()` and fill it up with `TitleId`, a flag to create a new account, and unique identifier. In our case, we can use the one given from `SystemInfo` as an identifier. Then, we need to make the call, and we check whether it is a new user or not with a couple of `if` statements:

```
void Login(string titleId) {
    LoginWithCustomIDRequest request = new LoginWithCustomIDRequest() {
        TitleId = titleId,
        CreateAccount = true,
        CustomId = SystemInfo.deviceUniqueIdentifier
    };
```

```
PlayFabClientAPI.LoginWithCustomID(request, (result) => {
    PlayFabId = result.PlayFabId;
    Debug.Log("The PlayFabID is: " + PlayFabId);

    if (result.NewlyCreated) {
        Debug.Log("new account has been created");
    }
    else {
        Debug.Log("Logged in with an existing account");
    }
},
(error) => {
    Debug.Log("An error occured");
    Debug.Log(error.ErrorMessage);
});
}
```

Save the script, and if you wish, test it.

Exchanging data

Once we have the login working, the next step is to exchange data with the database. The Playfab API is extensive, and we cannot cover it all in this short paragraph. The following is a list of the common API calls:

- GetLeaderboard
- SendPushNotification
- GetPlayerStatistics
- GetCharacterInventory
- ConsumeItem
- AddFriend
- AddUserVirtualCurrency

However, I encourage you to check out the official documentation, where you can find the basics of exchanging data with the database:

```
https://api.playfab.com/docs/using-player-data
```

Summary

In this chapter, we have covered the process of playtesting as well as ways to go about it. This includes deciding what you want out of your playtest, where to playtest, and what to ask your playtesters. Then, we looked at how to take this information and use it to improve your game or application. Finally, we learned what data persistence is within our application and how to use `PlayerPrefs` to save data. Furthermore, we learned why databases are important for playtesting, how to install them, and how to use PlayFab to store our data in an online database.

In the next chapter, we will wrap up everything we did as part of the project. We will make sure that the project is ready to be published and that you have all of the necessary skills to get it to the final stage.

9
Graduating Your Project to Completion

We're almost there. The finish line is visible, and this chapter is about putting in those last efforts to achieve something wonderful. So, how do we go about finishing the application, making sure that there are no loose ends, bugs, or any oversights that will impact the final build? In this chapter, we will cover the following topics:

- To begin, *Finishing the application* will explore what is required to finish your application
- Next, we will look at *Optimizing the project for a mobile platform*, where we will learn how to optimize our application in many different ways, such as screen resolution, devices, and so on
- Then, before finishing up, *Getting it ready to publish* will cover the final things to consider before you press the *publish* button
- Lastly, *Where do I begin?* and *Towards new horizons* will consider the different additions to implement to the application to extend its functionality

Now that we have the outline for the penultimate chapter, we are ready to start getting our first application ready!

Finishing the application

We are almost there: now it is time to add the finishing touches and to send our gamified application out there into the wilderness. But before we do just that, there are some things that we need to consider. Some of the main issues that we will cover later in this chapter includes a *lack of optimization* (graphics, assets, code), *failing to test the application enough* and *diversely*, and *not having enough time to market it properly*. The biggest issue is that a game designer discovers this all too late in the process and, as a result, delays occur, and resources, time, money, and energy are wasted. Here are some things to consider when getting your project ready for publishing. Of course, these can be applied to all levels of the development process.

Optimizing the project for a mobile platform

There are many different ways to optimize a game for a mobile platform. Whether it is for a mobile or tablet, there are a few key things to consider, which we will discuss here.

> Unity provides a great resource for optimizing for mobile platforms
> docs.unity3d.com/Manual/MobileOptimizationPracticalGuide.html.
> This section also provides a list of other, more specific optimizations, such as scripts and graphics.

Processing the power

Let's look at the issues that can impede your gaming experience. Mobile devices (and computers in general) have limits on how much they can process at any one time, and ultimately, this impacts the performance of your game on a device. Some parts of your game can be extremely draining and, as a result, the running of your game is not as smooth as it could be. There are different things to consider for 2D and 3D games, and we're going to explore both in the following sections.

For 2D games

Some image formats can result in issues, especially in file size. If for some reason you have large image files, you can reduce the file size in a number of ways:

- Change the image resolution
- Change the image type

In Unity, you can change these in the importing settings. We encountered this screen in Chapter 6, in the *The Import Settings* section. Just select an asset from your `Project` folder and the following screen will appear:

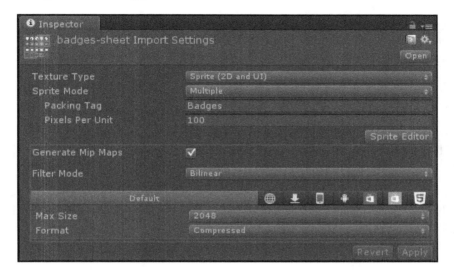

To improve the performance, the most important parameters are **Generate Mip Maps**, **Filter Mode**, **Max Size**, and **Format**. For your convenience, they have been highlighted in the screenshot.

Generate Mip Maps is an option that, if checked, creates smaller versions of the texture/sprite so, that when the sprite is far away or small with respect to the camera, a smaller version is rendered, improving performance. However, some people prefer to leave this unchecked so as not to alter the quality of their assets.

Filter Mode allows you to apply a filter to the image, in particular to make the borders a little bit blurry. When working with pixel art, having a filter on could be handy, since the filter makes your asset less *pixeled*. The official documentation says that **Filter Mode** selects how the texture is filtered when it gets stretched by transformations:

- **Point**: The texture becomes blocky up close.
- **Bilinear**: The texture becomes blurry up close.
- **Trilinear**: Like Bilinear, but the texture also blurs between the different map levels.

- **Max Size**: As the name suggests, the caps the maximum size that the image could have within that specific platform. In fact, artists often love to have high-resolution pictures or graphics, but sometimes it's not the best things for performance.
- **Format**: Specifies if the image will be compressed or not when the game is compiled/built. Keep in mind that if your target device is really old, it may not support some compressions formats.

For 3D games

This is going to be your nemesis if you're creating a 3D application. Poly counts are the number of faces that your 3D assets have. The cumulative total is what needs to be kept in consideration.

In the User Manual for Unity, there is a section that explains how to model assets and characters to achieve optimal performance. You can access this information via the following link:

```
http://polycount.com/discussion/130371/polygon-count-for-smartphone-application
s
```

To simply check the poly count inside your Unity scene, head to the top right corner of the **Game** view, and click on the **Stats** option, as seen in the following screenshot:

Once you have done this, a popup like the following screenshot should appear. Stats shows you a lot of performance information, such as draw calls, and indicates how many polygons are present in your current view of the scene. In fact, one of the great advantages of the Stats screen is that you can use it in real time when you press Play:

Other considerations

Another consideration is to reduce the number of materials in 3D assets. The less is more theory applies here and should be a mantra for the development of mobile games and applications. Mobile devices are capable of handling some pretty cool things, but everything has a limit, so keep this in mind as you begin to develop assets. Some materials could be really expensive from a computational point of view. There are shaders that replicate cool effects with a good approximation, and are optimized for mobiles.

Another way to reduce the number of polygons in Unity is by removing assets from the scene. This is not always possible, but it can be the first step before having to go back into your 3D graphics program. However, you can always remove some props from your level if you have exaggerated the number. The poly count is the number of faces that your 3D assets have. The cumulative total is what needs to be considered. In any case, if you want to dig deeper in graphics optimization in Unity, as always a good start is its official documentation:

```
https://docs.unity3d.com/Manual/OptimizingGraphicsPerformance.html
```

Test, test, and test again

Did I mention that you need to test? Not only test with your target, but test, test, and test again. Despite it being an obvious part of the overall process, this stage cannot be emphasized enough. Make sure that the game works on high-end *and* low-end devices. In fact, *make sure that it can run on ALL devices*. During this stage, it is ideal to keep a record of what has or hasn't worked. If during the test you find an interim solution to get by, note it down. If something happens once, but not twice during a playtest, try to recreate it.

At this stage, you don't want to assume that it *will* work for everyone if it works on your or your friends, tablet or phone. There have been cases where games don't run for a specific phone model, and on others they work very slowly. It can be difficult and probably an impossible feat to test on *all* devices, but if you have the chance, test on as many as possible. You can also refer to Chapter 7, *Get Your Motor Running*, for more information about playtesting and testing your game.

Don't have access to many devices? Not a problem

Ideally, it is better to test it out there in the flesh on a real phone, but if you can't, there are emulators. Genymotion is a product that offers a great way to emulate different devices: www.genymotion.com.

 Remember that some phones and mobile devices can practically run anything and everything, but others, not so much. Your consumers are going to have a range of devices from your basic smart phone to high-end phones with quad core processors.

Getting it ready to publish

So, you have finally finished making your game, and it is now time to hit the *publish* button…but wait! There are a number of things that you need have done before publishing, despite how tempting it is to unleash your game out there in the wilderness.

Don't be modest, promote your game!

Don't wait until you have published your game before you start telling people about it. Think about a marketing plan early on and get the ball rolling and the conversation started. Social media such as Twitter, Instagram, Facebook, and even blogs if you don't have a website, are useful platforms to utilize.

While there is still time before you publish your game, starting early will make the most impact. This section will briefly explain a range of different social networking services and ways to utilize their features as part of your marketing strategies.

- **Get popular**: Remember in school there were those *popular* kids who knew everyone and everything? Well, the same thing exists in social networks, and especially in games. Take a moment to get to know who's who. Know who the influences are within your specific area, and try to reach out. Reaching out does not mean spamming them, but genuinely and honestly ask them for their help. This can be something as simple as a tweet or as detailed as an e-mail. To keep track of your *social score*, you can use Klout (`www.klout.com`), which provides you with a score, or rather *rating*, between 1 and 100 based on social media analytics.
- **Becoming official**: If you already have a solid build for your game, try pitching it to popular blogs and websites. Perhaps your game helps individuals manage their diabetes in a new and innovative way. The idea is to get it featured on their website to gain a bit of traction and stir up some interest.

Sharing is caring

The way you sell your game can be important to its success. Of course, a large part of it all has to do with the game actually being good, but it doesn't hurt to *sell it*. Here are some ideas to use with social networking services as part of your marketing plan to get your game out there and build a bit of momentum before you publish. The great part of all of this is it can literally cost you nothing (except time, of course) to promote your game.

Facebook

Facebook offers a range of different features for advertisements and opportunities to connect with your audience:

1. **Pages**: Create a page and populate it a bit before making it public. People don't want to come to an empty page, so give them a reason to stay. There are different ways to get visitors engaged, from an interesting read to an eye-catching photo. Which one is more beneficial will depend on what you want to achieve.

2. **Posts**: Posts can be utilized in many ways. Given that Facebook offers four different ways to interact with a post, like, comment, tag, or share, each can be used in ways outside these explicit functions. For example, if you're asking about a particular component for the game, such as a color scheme, you could ask them to *like* for option one, *comment* for option two, and *share* for option three. For option two, you can encourage them to *tag* their friends as part of the process. This all works twofold: while you get them interacting with your posts, you're also getting a small portion of publicity from it all. For example, each time a user *shares* the post, it's being displayed within the *sharer's* network, and thus reaching more potential users.

3. **Polls**: Polls can be used as a way to quickly gauge users' opinions. This is a bit more direct than the methods explained previously. Of course, you can use polls to encourage competitive behavior such as *the winning choice will be implemented in our next game.*

4. **Live**: Facebook's *live* feature allows you to stream an event in real time, so why not take advantage of it and demo some *live game development* or a *Q&A*? This kind of setting allows your audience to connect with you and your team.

Twitter

Keeping it short, sharp, and to the point is what Twitter is all about. Twitter is a lively fast-paced environment that allows news to be featured as it happens, or in short updates:

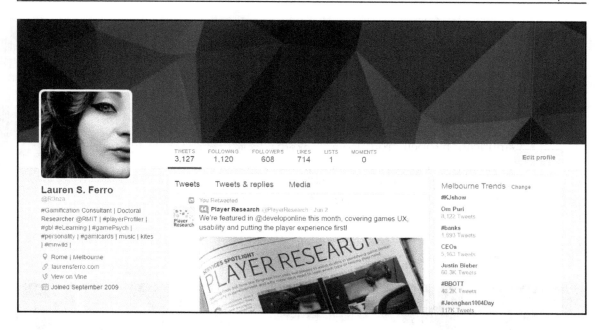

- **Tweeting**: There are a number of things to keep in mind when you are tweeting updates about your application, some of which, such as the time zone, we will cover later. However, Twitter uses a few key methods of interaction: reply, retweet, quote, favorite, and hashtags. Now, reply, as the name suggests, allows users to reply to what you have posted. This allows you to keep in touch with those who are interested. Retweeting is Twitter's version of *sharing*, and *favorites* is similar to *like*. Therefore, as mentioned before, you can use these in the same way to interact with your audience and to expand your content across different users. Hashtags, on the other hand, are probably one of the most fundamental things to keep in mind when sharing content. Using unique hashtags helps you to not only keep track of content distribution that is related to your game, but it also makes it easier to be heard and not lost among other *tweets*.

A great way to ensure that your hashtag is unique is to search it before using it.

- **Periscope**: Similar to Facebook Live, periscope allows Twitter users to Tweet live. Perhaps your audience is curious to see how you create the music for your game? Periscope it! Give them a teaser, and get them to come back for more!

LinkedIn

To target a more professional market, LinkedIn allows you to interact directly with your professional network. This can be particularly useful if you're part of groups or connected with people who are within the area that you are intending to target.

Some groups to get you started are as follows:

- Gamification (open group) www.linkedin.com/groups/4593540
- Gamification: higher engagement in education www.linkedin.com/groups/4959183
- People in games www.linkedin.com/groups/1818270
- Game Developers www.linkedin.com/groups/59205
- Serious Games Group www.linkedin.com/groups/137156
- Gamification www.linkedin.com/groups/3083943

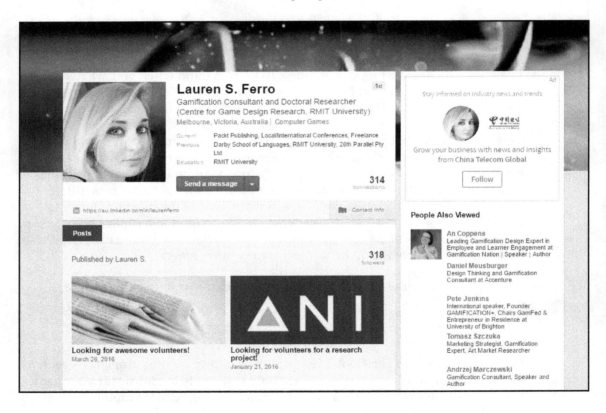

Instagram

Instagram can be a great platform to post images, as seen in the following screenshot, to keep users engaged with all the image aspects of your project:

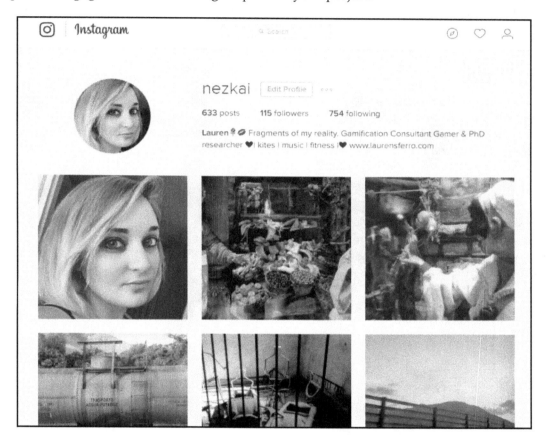

Snapchat and Vine

They say that a picture is worth a thousand words, so a short movie must tell volumes. Snapchat keeps things interesting with videos that are only available for a limited time, whereas Vine plays videos within a loop. Both are useful platforms to utilize and don't require a lot of time commitment.

YouTube

Video is a great way to explain to your audience about changes or updates to your game either post-publication or pre-publication. One of the great things about video is that it can be a bit more personal in terms of how you are able to present yourself. Text, audio, and images can convey a range of different opinions, and express many emotions, but nothing sums it all up like a nicely done video.

Blogs and websites

Blogs such as Tumblr and Blogger, among others, are great platforms to write longer posts about what is happening during the development process. See the following image of an example of Tumblr. These blogs are pretty simple to get started with and they can connect to a wide audience:

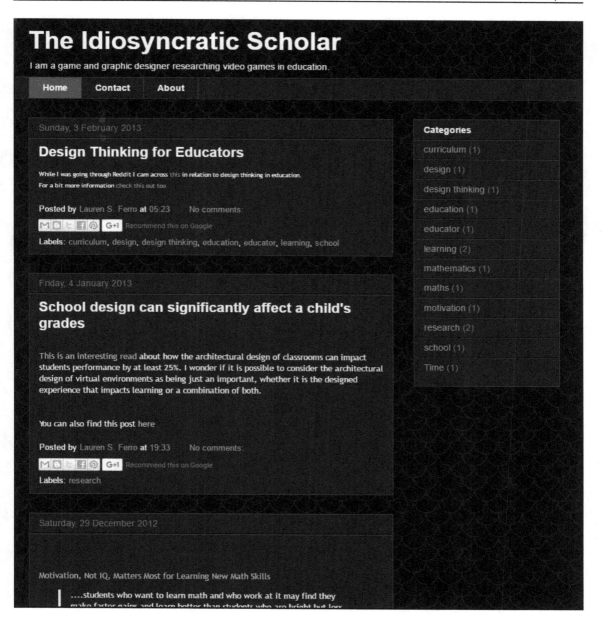

Documenting the process

During development, many designers keep a development diary (also known as a dev diary). Just like one would keep a journal, full of thoughts, drawings, ideas, and so on, a dev diary works in the same way. As you develop your application, write a post, write something about a new feature, or a new aspect of your application. Perhaps introduce your team along the way so that people can have an idea about the people who are part of the game.

Describing updates

While all of the social networking platforms tend to cycle through new information at a faster rate than blogs, blogs allow you to explain things in more detail. This is where the juice is and where you can really reach out to your audience. Describe a new update in detail, how you came up with it, when, where, and how you're going to implement it. When I say detail, you don't have to go into granular aspects.

MailChimp

If you don't have the time or resources to be constantly updating, then newsletters (and in turn, mailing lists) are a great way to let those who are interested know when cool things happen. Newsletters can be about different things, and feature different aspects of the project. They can contain news about different members such as *meet the programmer* to keep readers involved and feel like part of the team.

Paying attention to statistics

Many social networking platforms provide a section with statistics relating to various parts of the network, such as in the following screenshot (Twitter's analytic page). For example, every time you post something, you can find out how many people it reached, how many times it got shared and when, and then compare it to other statistics:

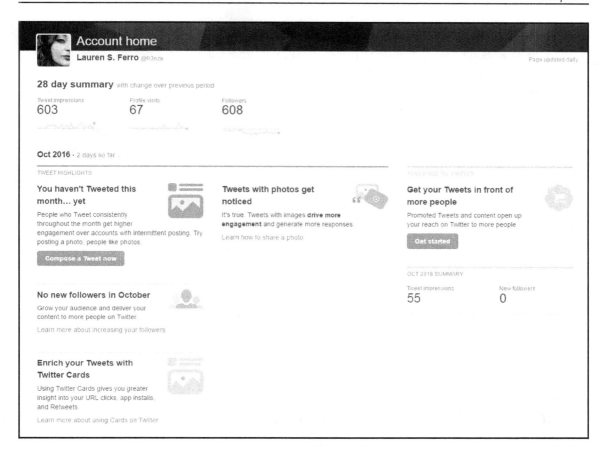

Engaging with your audience

If you're documenting the process, ask those who are engaging with your content for their opinions. Create polls, post questions, and ask for their responses.

Rewarding engagement

Sites such as Kickstarter, Indiegogo, and so on all provide rewards for certain levels of commitment from their project backers. You can adopt similar approaches to the development and eventual release of your game:

- **Competitions**: Running competitions is a great way to get people involved. If you don't have the funds to create products, offer full versions of your game. Another option is to create some exclusive artwork/wallpapers and, if possible, get them printed.
- **Network distribution**: During competitions, instead of asking people to just *write a comment* in response to your question, get them to *like*, *share*, and even *tag* friends as part of the process or as a condition for entering the competition. It's a win-win situation: they have the potential to gain something for free, you have publicized your game across many potential networks outside those that you are targeting on your own.
- **Feedback**: Feedback is gold when it comes to making sure your game is as good as it can be. When people give you detailed feedback, they take time out of their days and commit it to helping you. In most cases, even negative feedback when it's constructively critical is important to consider and even implement during the iterative stages. Therefore, while feedback tends to be altruistic, reward those who make an effort.

It's a hoot! Managing social networks

Managing one time zone is hard; managing multiple time zones can be a real challenge if you're not organized, especially if you are using many different social networks. The sections here describe different approaches to handling it all. These programs also allow you to schedule posts in the future.

 If you're planning on having many social networking platforms, then it is worthwhile taking the time to find a good social networking manager. Here are some suggestions:

- Hootsuite https://hootsuite.com/
- IFTT https://ifttt.com/
- Buffer https://buffer.com/

Remembering time zones

Your audience is not going to be located in any one place, unless you're targeting a very specific audience. Therefore, you need to remember that there are 24 time zones and you need to reach them all somehow. A good way to ensure that you cover all the continents is to tweet the same info at least four times a day. But to avoid repetition, try to mix it up a bit, either by changing the post slightly or by posting other things in between. For example, if you're posting about a new dev diary post, follow it up with a post (or repost) from Instagram, or a link to your Facebook page. The last most important thing to keep in mind is, if you run competitions or anything that is time-sensitive, always put in the time zone, for example, *Check back here at 10:30am (GMT +2) for our live interview. Don't miss it!* A great online tool to quickly manage this is World Time Buddy, `http://www.worldtimebuddy.com`. An example of it is shown in the following screenshot:

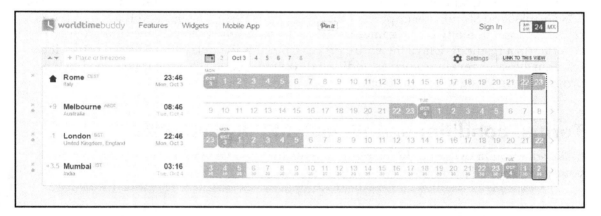

There are many great applications that manage time zones around the world, so be sure to have one. Ideally, you want to post to each continent at an ideal time. For example, commute times and lunch are perfect times to schedule posts. Chances are, for the most part, they won't be looking at their feeds while working.

Tag! You're it

With so many social networks, it can be hard to be heard amongst the noise of every other game developer. Therefore, we are lucky that tags, better known as hashtags, exist. While posting on social networking services helps us be heard, using hashtags helps us to be heard by those that we need to listen. It is the difference between going to a supermarket and asking for bread or going to a bakery. They both have audiences, but one is more specific than the other. It is worthwhile taking the time to see how other developers and publishers that produce games that are similar to yours tag their posts.

Getting commercial

If you're planning on uploading your application on either Android (Google Play Store) or iOS (Apple App Store), it is important that you review their policies and that your game respects those. In many cases, games get rejected for failing to meet some fundamental criteria. As a result, it delays the entire process. Besides the delay that this can cause, it can result in a loss of revenue, such as additional costs for fixing the issue if you need to hire programmers, designers, and so on.

Terms, conditions, policies, and agreements

Make sure you know not only the requirements that you need to meet in order to upload your game, but also that your game adheres to them.

The publishing checklist

Here is a simple checklist to ensure that you have the basics sorted when it comes to publishing your game on their relevant app stores:

1. Check the size of the application.
2. Check to see if your game adheres to the terms and conditions, and/or policies for the store.
3. Test on a range of difference devices.
4. Verify that images/assets have been optimized.
5. Verify that it works. This goes without saying, but it is still overlooked more than people think.

Now it's time to press the Build button

Finally, it's time to actually build the game. It can be done by clicking on **File** | **Build Settings…**. The following screen appears:

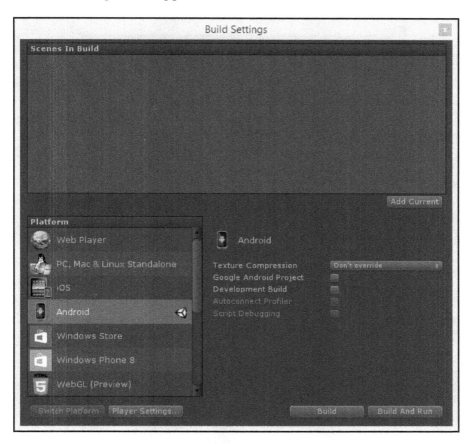

Before we build, we need to add a scene. In the project we developed during this book, we only have one scene, so we can add it by clicking on **Add Current**. Then, we need to specify a platform; in our case, we can pick Android. If you want to really go deeper into the settings, you can press the **Player Settings...** button, and you will see this screen in the **Inspector**:

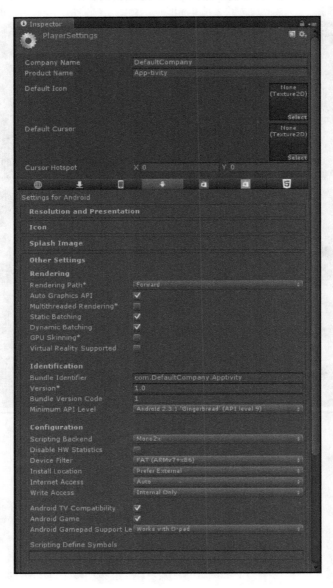

Here, you can granularly set how your game will be exported. In our case, for Android, it's really important to set an identifier, otherwise Unity won't allow us to export the game. To do this, click on the **Other Settings** tab, if it's not already opened, and navigate to **Bundle Identifier** in the **Identification** section. For your convenience, it is highlighted in the following screenshot:

We are developing for Android in this book; if you are looking for more information regarding developing for iOS, the official Unity documentation is a great place to start:

- Getting started with iOS development: `https://docs.unity3d.com/Manual/iphone-GettingStarted.html`
- Building your Unity game to an iOS device for testing: `https://unity3d.com/learn/tutorials/topics/mobile-touch/building-your-unity-game-ios-device-testing`
- Manual: Unity iOS Basics: `https://docs.unity3d.com/Manual/iphone-basic.html`

We can type, as in the screenshot, `com.DefaultCompany.Apptivity`. This will be a unique identifier for your application. The parameters will make the build unique as well. With regard to the other settings, we can just leave the defaults in place. However, if you are interested in learning more, you can check the official documentation here:

`http://docs.unity3d.com/Manual/class-PlayerSettings.html`

Finally, go back to the previous screen and press **Build**. Unity will ask us where to save it. Congratulations, you got your gamified application exported!

Where do I begin?

So, we have covered quite a large amount of content and ways to approach social media, marketing, and getting your application ready for publishing, so where do you begin?

Short-term

In the short term, it is important to keep active. That way, even if your development process takes time, people are reminded about the awesome work that you are doing. Short posts about what you're up to, or an image during the development process, are all enough to maintain interest, but not to indefinitely keep it. Make sure that you have more detailed updates along the way so that there is a bit more context about what you and your team have been up to.

Long-term

Create a timeline, such as in the following figure, from when you begin developing to when you will be finished. Ideally, you should already have a timeline, but if you don't, create one. In this timeline, include all the different stages, for example, iterations, testing, and so on, and approximate dates. Now, with this *timeline*, brainstorm some ideas for blog posts and articles. This is only a tentative list, because as the game develops, so too will ideas for posts. Now, once you are done, put it somewhere safe and remember to keep iterating it. As you begin to approach each section of the timeline, start to write your articles. If they can be done in advance, such as *meet the team*-type ones, then start early. By doing this, you will always have content to share and won't have to stay up all night writing blog posts:

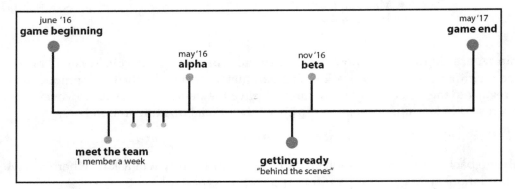

Another useful thing to have is a *press kit*. Think of this as an overview of your project along with accompanying material, such as logos and images, that will be used by the public (without any copyright issues) to promote your game. By having these things available, you ensure that, wherever your content is being distributed, they have high quality material and the right facts. It's also a good reference point when you need to quickly send a summary of your project.

Another thing is to always engage with your audience, ask them questions, ask for their feedback, and get them involved and caring about your game. Games need players, and we as game designers want players to be a part of the experience. People are curious about what goes on *behind the scenes*.

Towards new horizons

Just because we have finished the application in terms of what this book explains, it doesn't mean that there are no additional features that you can add at a later stage. To get an idea of other features to add, take a look back at the game elements list in `Chapter 1`, *The Anatomy of Games!* Think of different ways that you can incorporate the elements or mechanics to achieve the same result. For example, instead of a badge, give the player a higher status, or reveal another part of the story. Experimenting is the key when it comes to taking your ideas and evolving them!

Summary

This chapter covered different aspects of getting your application ready to publish. It included the marketing aspect, and different ways to engage your audience. It featured important things to consider before pressing *Publish*, such as making sure to adhere to the terms and conditions. We also discussed short- to long-term planning for the time leading up to publishing. Lastly, this chapter recommends considering new game elements to implement into the current application to give it some alternate gameplay features.

Our next chapter will be our last, and it will complete our journey. But of course, just because this book has come to an end, it doesn't mean your journey into the world of gamification has to, so get ready to find out how you can develop your skills in other ways and develop the skills that you have learned in this book. Exciting adventures await!

10
Being the Best That You Can Be!

Congratulations! You have made it to the final chapter! This is itself worthy of a celebration. But before we bring out the cake, and embark on such festivities, we have a few more things to cover. More specifically, we will cover the following topics in our final moments together:

- To begin, *Getting your game on without overdoing it*, will explain important elements of the design process to keep in mind in order to extend the design of your application. In addition, it will explain a range of useful, essential, and practical approaches to designing gamified experiences.
- We will proceed by discussing *New and future directions* that will cover the ways that what we have learned can be used within the application and how our application can impact real life in a more influential way. In addition, it will discuss additional ways to develop the design of your application.
- Lastly, we will conclude this chapter, and our gamified journey, with *Improving your skills once you have finished reading this book*, which will explain as well as provide a list of resources to explore once you have learned everything that there is learn within this book.

Getting your game on without overdoing it

During the process of designing gamified applications, the motto that you should keep in mind is *just because you can, doesn't mean you should*, especially when you begin to add badges, points, and so on to your experience. Badges and points are not the answer to all motivational problems, just like gamification is not going to be the magic dust that you have been looking for to fix a broken system. The other consideration is to not think that gamification is like an additional layer to add to an existing system. In some cases, it is possible to integrate the two, so that one system that is already in place blends in with the new gamified approach, but it does require some work.

Understand what gamification is and what it is not

Many times, people assume that anything gamified is *fun* and that making tests digital is turning them into a game. Unfortunately, both those ideologies are false. For example, transforming multiple choice questions from requiring a student to color in a, b, c, or d on an answer sheet into checkboxes or radio buttons is not making it a game. Gamification is quantifying and acknowledging tasks within a set of rules. How playful it is is up to you. It is not making something digital (for example, written tests to digital ones) and it most certainly does not guarantee that it will be fun. Fun, pleasure, amusement, entertainment, and enjoyment are all relative emotions. To some extent, we all share common activities that we find fun or enjoyable, such as watching a movie, but even then, some people prefer science fiction, and others, comedy. Therefore, it is important to understand the difference between how gaming experiences are fun for us, and how they differ, and that if you think it is fun, it doesn't mean it will be for others. In addition, learn and understand how motivation works and doesn't work. If you want long-term engagement but you're really only facilitating external reinforcement, then you're likely to run into issues.

Kids see through chocolate covered broccoli, and so do adults

We all know the term *a wolf in sheep's clothing,* or think that covering vegetables in decadent chocolate will get them to be healthy and, well, kids are a lot more perceptive than we sometimes give them credit for. If you disguise educational content with gameplay, it is likely that they will see through it. This isn't related to children; the same is true with adults. We know that by using a gamified application we intend to monitor our health or spending habits, but it's your job as a designer to make it a little less painful. Therefore, be upfront, transparent, and cut through the *disguise* and focus on the benefits. Of course, kids don't want to be asked to *play a game about maths,* but they are going to be more interested in *going on adventures to beat the evil dragon with trigonometry.* The same goes for adults; creating an awesome character that can be upgraded to a level 80 warrior for remembering to take out the trash, keep hydrated, and eat healthier is a lot better than telling them this is a *fun* application to become a better person.

Using gamification in moderation

When creating gamified applications, it can be tempting to *gamify all the things...*but don't. If the term gamification is synonymous with badges and points for you, then you have some learning to do. For this reason, a list of different game elements and mechanics are described in `Chapter 1`, *The Anatomy of Games.* Every good gamification designer looks beyond the game's elements and mechanics; they focus on the changes that they want their end user to make.

Getting tangential

Gamification allows us to merge games and reality, and this is a perfect opportunity to encourage tangential learning. Tangential learning is planting the *seed* in someone's mind about a topic, that they then on their own go and investigate to learn more about. A perfect example of this is in the game Assassin's Creed. Playing the game, even the series, exposes the player to some historical periods of time, such as the Third Crusade or the American Revolution. Some other games that achieve this are Sid Meier's Civilization series and Portal, as seen in the following screenshots from the game:

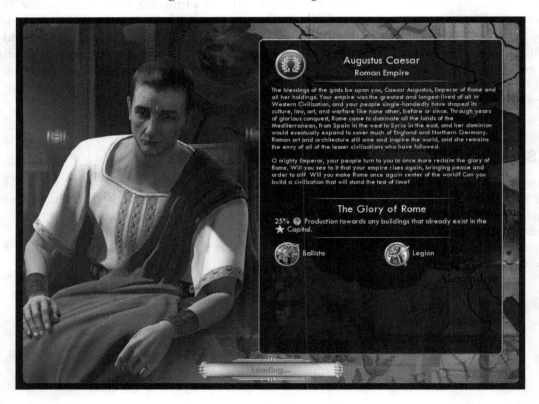

Sid Meier's Civilization V, www.civilization5.com

Based on this, an example of the process of tangential learning is presented in the following screenshot. In this example, the user engages with the game Civilization V, and assumes the role of Augustus Caesar:

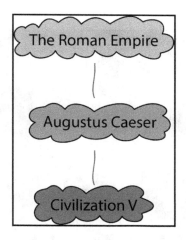

In the case of Portal and Portal 2, the gameplay that allows players to interact using various types of physics such as momentum, acceleration (if you jump into a portal from a high distance), as well as different substances (Portal 2), encourages children to also find out more about them. For example, the concept of *portals* in itself is heavily based on a number of different concepts of physics, as well as varying opinions, which is something any student can find out by simplifying exploring search results stemming from a simple search of *portal* in Google. In addition, the different substances that feature in Portal 2 can reduce or create friction, which allows players to complete certain tasks. Something as simple as different substances demonstrates the different effects that they have, which adds another dimension than reading from a text book:

If you're interested in seeing the concept of the sprayable substances, check out the game tag, the power of Paint, here: www.tinyurl.com/TagTheGame

Portal 2, www.store.steampowered.com/app/400

Be prepared to fail

Game development is hard and time-consuming work. Never underestimate the time that it takes to implement something. Generally, if you need to add a new feature, multiply the estimated amount that it will take by about three. For example, if you think a new level will take one week, set aside three weeks. That way, if something goes wrong, which it can and does, you will have additional time to fix it without being pressed with a deadline. If your deliver earlier than expected, that's great, move on to the next item in the list.

Test it!

I really, really, cannot make this point clear enough. Test your game at *every* stage, especially once it becomes digital. Test it on any and every device that you can, and with as many people as possible. Did I mention to test your game? Remember to refer to `Chapter 8`, *Break, Destroy, and Rebuild – the Art of Playtesting and Iteration*, during the stages of testing to make sure that you're addressing the essentials:

Feel free to photocopy this badge, print it out (if you have the eBook), and cut it out. Stick it on your computer, fridge, anywhere so that you don't forget this step!

The iterative cycle

If it doesn't work, fix it; if it does, can it be improved? Each time you test your game, pay attention to feedback and to the flow of your game. If something doesn't feel right to you, the chances are it won't to your players. Treat each stage of the iterative process as a stage of refinement, like the details being carved into a sculpture. Remember that it is okay to change things at this stage, because it refines your application. If you check out `Chapter 8`, *Break, Destroy and Rebuild – the Art of Playtesting and Iteration*, you can find a lot more information about the process in more detail.

Backup...everywhere

Backups are right up there next to testing on the broken record of game development. An important lesson I learned from my high school IT teacher was that not only should you backup on a USB, hard drive, cloud, but do it all, more than once and in more than one location!

What happens if your only backup was on the cloud and then one day, it's gone? Or you only backed up the data on your laptop and then one day it just stopped working? Or, you backed up your project only on external hard drives, but all in the same location and then it all burned down. By now, you should get the point: have multiple backups in different locations, both physical and virtual, and make sure that they all have the most recent files. Having a backup from five months ago on your only functioning backup is not going to be entirely useful a week from your publishing date.

If backup isn't enough, there are version control tools. These allow you to keep track of the changes in your projects, and branch them, allowing you to work in parallel to then merge them together again. These are really powerful tools; however, it takes a little to enter their logic and set them up properly at the beginning. Unluckily, we don't have time to go in detail in source control tools, but it's worth mentioning that the most commonly used is Git. If you search on Google, you can find different guides that teach you different parts of Git. In any case, there are some free services online to post a repository, and starting to play with them helps you to understand Git better as well. The most famous one is GitHub, and here is a beginner guide: `https://guides.github.com/activities/hello-world/`.

Another thing when it comes to backups is keeping the names of your files consistent. For example, `image_final.png` and `image_final_final.png` are not ideal ways to let team members and clients know what is the current version. Whether you have an underscore `_` or not in your naming convention is also up to you, but if you decide to use them, keep on using them. Lastly, although this goes without saying, keep the names short but meaningful. For example, `image.png` is not extremely descriptive, whereas `background_image_login_screen.png` is. I have found that naming conventions for a project are best outlined in the GDD. Since it is a shared document, and everyone has to read it, it is the most ideal and central place for team members to refer to during the design process.

Before we finish our overview of the backup process, here is a list of different tools to get your backups underway, and keep your future self happy if any issues arise:

- USBs and (external) hard drives are the old-school methods of backing up data. They provide you with a physical option for backing up your precious data. Remember, if you only plan on using physical devices, keep a copy of the file on around three different devices, in different (on-site and off-site) locations.
- Servers are an option if you have the hardware to create your own or have someone do it for you. It is relatively simple, but if you're planning on it becoming a permanent thing, make sure that it's also a cost-effective venture (remember, servers require electricity and constant up-time). One of the benefits is that you can have a large, secure server just for yourself without the worry of having to pay for additional storage (except if you need to buy a new hard drive for additional space).
- Dropbox (`www.dropbox.com`) and Google Drive (`www.drive.google.com`) allow you to back up your data to an online server, providing that you have created an account. In both cases, they offer a generous amount of space to store your files, but if you find that it is not enough, then you will need to purchase more.

Teamwork...play nice

Consideration, collaboration, and communication are all important during the game development process. Working environments should be free from the sense of *punishment* of other team members, and to ensure this you need to keep all lines of communication open. While it may seem obvious, a tiny problem such as not knowing how to do something, if communicated early on, reduces stress when everyone is expecting it at a later stage. Game development groups all have different levels of expertise; therefore, we may be capable of many things or a few things. Have this conversation early on so that, there are no assumptions, and so that if a part of the project needs to be outsourced, it can be done and on time. If you can't do something, it is fine, but don't over-promise and under-deliver.

One way to visualize your work schedule is with a **Gantt Chart**, such as in the following figure. In this way, members of the team can see processes that can be done in parallel with each other, and ones that may require the completion of another before starting:

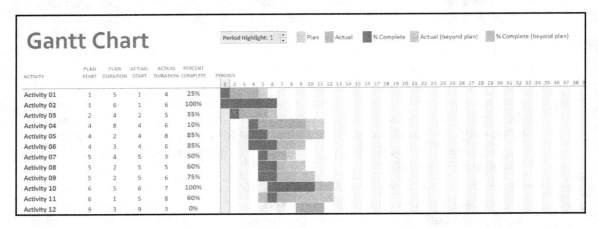

An example of a Gantt Chart using Microsoft Excel's (https://www.microsoftstore.com/store/msin/en_GB/pdp/Excel-2016/productID.324412900) Gantt Chart template

Now that the lines of communication are open, keep in mind that people have lives outside your project. Sometimes it is easy to be so focused on the end goal that we forget this. In other cases, we have more time than others and assume that they are also free to work. However, the programmer in your group, he may have a newborn, a mortgage to pay off, and work a second job; therefore, asking him to commit his entire weekend to the project at the last minute is probably not going to end well. So, be mindful that unless everyone is *full-time* on your project, and maintaining a steady income because of it, you need work around each other. Another consideration is also the tasks that are being implemented. In some cases, they are small, quick things that take a few hours to complete; others may be more complicated, and even the most competent person struggles with them. Therefore, unless you have a team with experienced experts in your team, keep this in mind.

New and future directions

Everything that we have covered in this book, as well as the application itself, will provide you with a foundation to base any number of gamified approaches on, some of which are discussed in the following section. Of course, remember that gamified applications and approaches don't always have to be digital, and they shouldn't just be about badges, points, and rewards. A gamified experience should be considered as a complementary resource, something that gives you that extra kick when you really just can't be bothered, not something that is relied upon.

Uses within education

Using gamification in education is a topic with many different opinions, which would require an entire book or two to cover. However, you can use what you have learned in the book and apply it within an educational context. Some examples are listed in the following section, but I encourage you to explore what others have done throughout the world and be inspired.

Homework management

Kids don't generally like homework unless there is something that they find interesting about it. Some ideas that you could use are to allow children to set tasks, or to choose from a list of predefined ones and then complete them. For example, if they have biology homework that needs to be completed, get them to break it down into chunks, and if they complete it all within a certain time frame, they can go to the movies or maybe get that toy that they always wanted. If you want to spice things up a bit, you can always add a narrative or quests to give a bit more meaning to what they have to do. Maybe slay the *mitosis demon* by completing related homework.

Other ideas also include the following:

- Reading assignments (for example, chapter by chapter towards a badge, or reward)
- Studying for tests
- Getting good grades

There are a number of classroom activities that don't have to involve anything digital, and you can use to get your students a bit more engaged with lesson content. The following are a few ideas for you to try out within your classroom.

Who wants to be a knowledge-aire?

We have all seen the shows where someone is placed in a seat and faced with a question and four possible options. In most cases, they have a few ways to get assistance such as *phone a friend*, or *50/50*, and so on. Therefore, why not bring the same concept into the classroom? While classroom tests will still exist, this is an exciting way to get not only students involved in learning the content, but also producing it.

For example, for a class homework assignment, ask each student to write down a question with four possible answers about the current topic. This can be anything from a mathematics equation to a character from a play that is being studied. Students can e-mail them to you, bring them to class, and so on. However, the main thing is that they are also checked beforehand to make sure that they are correct. Once everything is sorted, randomly choose a student; you can do this by having them write their names on a piece of paper and *pull one out of the hat*. Then, they have to try and answer as many questions as possible within a time limit. You can implement options such as to *ask a friend* or *50/50*. The main thing to reinforce is that it is meant to be fun.

Hide and seek

Sometimes, content can be really boring, but one way to mix it up a bit is to give students something to search for. Example 1: if students have to read passages from a play, then create a quest for them such as deciphering a cryptic clue.

Example 2: if they are reading about trigonometry, perhaps the first number of each answer is part of the *secret* combination that the professor needs to free the triangles from an inevitable fate! Try to avoid getting them to search for simple things such as *the second word from paragraph 4 on page 21*. This will not encourage them to learn the content but to focus on the game, and the game is only a complementary component. Instead, you could still get them to find a particular word, but in a more indirect way. For example, the answer to question x reveals the page number, the answer to y reveals the number for the paragraph, and the answer to z reveals the number for word, and so on.

The ultimate race

To create a year-long challenge, you can get students to compete for a *mystery prize*; what that prize is, in the end, is up to you. Each lesson is a part of this race, and at any moment, a classroom task or homework assignment that is assessed could be contributing to this race. Ideally, each task that is included in this race contributes to it somehow. For example, one task may be worth five points: one point for starting it, two points for getting it right, and two points for finishing it. You could represent this race like a board game where students know when certain things will happen. However, to avoid them trying to game the system, the unknown creates much more excitement! Now, along the way, there must be something in place that determines the *winner*. This can be an *elimination round* where students are pressed against the time to answer as many questions as possible, or they could be eliminated for bad behavior, or something else. In reverse, students could be given additional points for arriving in class on time and good behavior.

Uses within business

A business context has many layers; you have your own day-to-day tasks as well as group/project-related ones. Sometimes it can be a bit overwhelming, and as a result, stress and anxiety levels increase. One way to add a bit more *life* to some otherwise mundane tasks.

Other ideas also include the following:

- **Productivity**: This can include anything from meeting deadlines to submitting reports on time. One of the key areas to identify when creating a gamified experience to encourage productivity is why it's becoming an issue in the first place. If it is something to do with the work environment, creating a reward scheme isn't going to solve the problem. A few examples of productivity applications include the following:
    - Habit RPG (as already discussed in `Chapter 1`, *The Anatomy of Games*): www.habitrpg.com
    - Mind Bloom: www.mindbloom.com
    - Time Tune: www.timetune.center

- **Punctuality/efficiency**: *Time is money*, and if you can reduce the time that it takes to do something, such as arriving at work or completing a project, you are likely to reap more benefits in the long run. However, again, like productivity, the key is to identify the issues causing a lack of promptness and to find ways to prevent it. Of course, we all like a pat on the back once in a while, and a gamified application can certainly achieve that!

- **Managing workloads**: Especially during busy times of the year such as the holiday season, we can be inundated with last-minute requests to get projects completed on time without them having to eat into our vacation time. One way is to create Gantt charts, but where is the fun in that? Finding creative ways to manage sometimes overwhelming workloads can be the key to keeping stress levels down, or at least reducing them.

- **Team management**: We all remember that project in school where we worked as part of the team, but ended up doing it ourselves...well, perhaps for the most part. Sometimes it can be difficult to work with people in a team, especially if you have opposing opinions, different lifestyles, all of which can impact a team's ability to work effectively. Therefore, incorporating a bit of playfulness can be a great way to break down any issues. An example of a team management related-application is Asana (www.asana.com).

However, just like work, our own lives away from the office can also benefit from gamified experiences. The following is a brief discussion about some other sub-contexts of personal uses for gamified applications.

Uses within personal life

There are many different parts of our lives that we have working as they should, and then there are others that we could use a bit of help with. Not everything is an experience that we may necessarily want to share with others; sometimes the urge to make the changes that we need to feel happy with ourselves, and with our lives in general, comes from within. These types of change include being healthier, fitter, more productive, and also better at organizing our lives so that we actually have one without it being overcome by work. Here is a list of different areas that gamified applications can be used for within our personal lives:

- **Increasing healthier habits**: When *one more donut* ended up being two or sometimes three, we could have made a better choice. But it's hard, and anyone who has made an attempt to stay on the healthy path knows that delicious cakes and tasty fried food takes us down the dark path of temptation to satisfy our taste buds. However, *where there is a will there is a way*, and being conscious about what we do (or shouldn't do but end up doing anyway) can help us make better decisions. Sometimes all it takes is a few extra points for eating less, a positive message after losing those extra five kilos, to make all the difference. Some examples of fitness-related applications include:
    - Zombies, Run! (as discussed in `Chapter 1`, *The Anatomy of Games*): `www.zombiesrungame.com`
    - Lifesum: `wwww.lifesum.com`
- **Maintaining a work/life balance**: It's the difference between having a hobby that is flying a kite, or crunching numbers on a weekend for the annual financial report, while everyone is at the beach. Drawing the line between work and life can be hard, especially if you work from home, or your job is unpredictable. However, it is possible to manage it all, at least in some way so we can allow ourselves some time to relax. Notifications that remind us to take a break, to go out and get some fresh air, perhaps even walk the dog, can all help us to break away from it all. Perhaps you want to begin yoga, or learn to surf; scheduling our lives is one way to go about it, but rewarding your efforts (100 points for placing yourself first!) for not bringing your work home can help you to leave some time for you and your family. An example of a work/life balance related application is **Atracker** (`www.wonderapps.se`).

- **Reducing bad habits**: We all succumb to something that we could make a better choice about, such as smoking, drinking soda every day, or not being as nice as we could. Therefore, why not try to encourage ourselves to make better choices, whether it's for ourselves, a loved one, or our family and friends. Sometimes, having a social support network that you can turn to for support, or compete against, can be enough to break the threshold and start the path to better habits. An example of a habit-related application is BreakFree (www.breakfree-app.com).

- **Chore/responsibility management**: Kids don't like chores…well, neither do adults. I love doing the washing, said no one ever, even though it's nice to have clean clothes. However, it is laborious, tedious, and a pain when you come home after working all day to find a sink full of dirty dishes that you said you would take care of yesterday. Therefore, gamified applications can at least make some part of the whole process fun. It's even possible to encourage a bit of healthy completion among members of the family or roommates, if there is a prize at stake! An example of a chore-related application is Chore Wars (www.chorewars.com).

- **Managing finances/taxes**: Nobody likes to do them (except for maybe accountants!), but we do like the tax return. So why, knowing that do we still struggle to do them? Well, they are boring, take a lot of concentration (if you do them yourself), and also require a bit of effort to keep things, such as receipts and invoices, organized throughout the year. Therefore, why not make a deal with yourself, or the application, that if you file it on time, even earlier than anticipated, you can indulge yourself a little. Perhaps you were bargaining with yourself whether or not to buy that pair of shoes, or that sound system that you have been eyeing all year; well, now's the chance! An example of a finance-related application is Smarty Pig (www.smartypig.com).

Of course, all of the applications previously mentioned are just suggested examples, and are not necessarily designed for that specific context. Therefore, take the time to check them out, and to also do a bit of research for yourself to find an application that works for you and can help you get to where you need to be.

Improving your skills once you have finished this book

Learning about the uses of gamification do not have to stop with his book. There are so many different resources available that extend what you have learned in this book as well as how to apply them. Here is a list of ways that you can go about extending your knowledge.

As a game design exercise, try using different techniques that have been described in this book to develop ideas to the previous suggestions within each context.

Become a researcher

You don't need a degree to research. Believe it or not, there are a lot of papers that are available that talk about new and innovative ways of creating game-like experiences. Not just papers, but conferences can also be great ways to get your game noticed too, especially if you're targeting areas such as STEM learning or health. They can be a bit expensive (in some cases, conference fees alone can range from $100-$600) depending on when, where, and how long they run for. However, if you have the opportunity to, they are definitely worthwhile. In some cases, conferences actually have a section dedicated to game development where you can submit your game. A great place to start finding useful papers is Google Scholar scholar.google.com, and a great place to find current and future game conferences is `http://www.gameconfs.com`.

Make design a daily habit

Go out right now, take this book with you, and find or buy a notebook. This will become your game design journal, for anything and everything game-related. Try and make a habit of writing down some game ideas every day, perhaps during breakfast, lunch, coffee break, or before you go to bed. This will become like a repository later when you might need some inspiration. There may be a part of a current game that you are designing that doesn't quite work, but something that you thought about, say, last week, can be the missing link. No idea is a bad idea; they all become useful at some point.

Another great idea is to make a list of all the games that you like. This list can be as large as you want it to be, and for each game, write a sentence about what you like and didn't like about the game. That way, when you reflect on these comments at a later stage, you can begin to mix ideas together. For example, what you didn't like in one game might complement something in another, and so on.

Redesigning your favorite games as board games

This activity I have done myself a number of times, and it actually gets you thinking and focusing on gameplay. The one thing that I admire about board games is that you cannot mask their gameplay with beautiful graphics, or amazing orchestral soundtracks (of course, you can play music in the background, though!) Breaking down games into parts, seeing how those parts interact with each other and how to represent them in a physical form, such as stones, counters, and so forth, will help you to gain a really good understanding of gameplay, and it's a fun process to do!

Never. Stop. Learning

Don't think that reading any one or number of books, or watching any number of tutorials will give you everything that you need to know. Each day, we are presented with new technologies, new methodologies, and as these become the latest trends, there are a bunch of researchers developing the technologies of tomorrow. Be sure to check the latest news on gamification both at a concept and its implementation within varying environments. As technology changes, so do the ways that people do things.

Play to win and play to explore

Now you have a legitimate excuse to game, which is *to learn*. By playing many different games across many different genres, you will not only be exposed to many different approaches that you can use for your own designs, but you will learn how to use them. There is more than one way to drink water, and there is definitely more than one way to give and get a badge. If you don't have a lot of time to play hour intense games, check out the latest mobile games, but whichever way you game, make sure you keep it in moderation and consistent.

What might also be worthwhile is to keep a game journal. In this journal, you can write about your experiences with games. What did you like/didn't you like? Was there something in particular that stood out that could be useful or even applied in a different way? You can also include color schemes, comments about music, and even the aesthetic style; include anything and everything that you find relevant. Remember that there is no right or wrong way to do it.

 A great web series that I recommend that you have a look at is the Extra Credits series. They discuss a whole range of topics related to games. You can find their videos here: www.youtube.com/user/ExtraCreditz.

Read game guides

While game guides are typically there to help you, you can definitely learn a thing or two about game design. While you are reading, pay attention to *how* players are expected to achieve certain tasks. Even if game guides are directed towards typical games and not necessarily gamified applications per se, it is possible to abstract them to gamified applications. The way that tasks are designed, how they reward the player can all be used to improve the implementation of the same or similar game elements into your application.

Participate, compete, and get together

There is a large range of gaming events, both local and around the world. Game jams are a great example of the participatory culture that games can offer. Some are short and last one day; others are long and last two or three days. But get involved and get in and amongst the community. Other opportunities such as meetups (www.meetup.com), game conventions, and conferences such as the Game Developer's Conference (www.gdconf.com), expos such as the EB Games Expo (www.ebexpo.com.au), Penny Arcade Expo (PAX, www.paxsite.com) and South by Southwest (SxSW, www.sxsw.com), and so forth, all offer other great opportunities to connect with other developers, gamers, and even an opportunity to showcase your work.

Summary

Congratulations! You have reached the end of this gamified adventure. In this chapter, we discussed the potential of using what you have learned within this book and applying it to other contexts. I hope that you have been inspired and this book has given you not just a better understanding not just of gamification in Unity, but also about the concept itself. There is still much to know and learn as this area, as well as approaches to it, are still developing.

Achievement unlocked!

Index

R

rapid prototyping 29
Ratio
    fixed reward schedules 56
    variable reward schedule 56
reinforcement
    examples 39, 40
resources, gamification 301
Roller-coaster Tycoon Series
    reference 50
rounded corners, badges
    creating, with Effect option 176, 178, 179
    creating, with Shape tool 174, 175

S

Scrum Alliance
    reference 108
scrum process
    working 105
Scrum
    reference 108
Scrumble
    reference 108
ScrumHub
    reference 108
Sennet game 8
serious games
    about 14
    America's Army 14
    Foldit 15
    Moonbase Alpha 15
Sid Meier's Civilization 12, 14
SimCity
    about 18
    reference 50
simulation games
    about 17, 18
    From Dust 19
    Virtual Heroes 17
Slatebox
    about 114
    reference 114
Smarty Pig
    reference 301

social networks
    hashtags 280
    managing 278
    time zones 279
SxSW
    reference 304
system, creating
    profile image, setting 70, 71, 72

T

Task class 217
Task Displayer 212
Task manager 225, 226
Task Panels 213
Tasks page
    setting up 238, 239
tasks
    about 165
    creation access, granting to user 227
    dealing with 219
    defining 216
    object-oriented language, working 216
    prefab, as Task panel 219, 220, 221, 222, 224
testers
    playing, observation 246
Third-Person Shooter (TPS) 10
Time Tune
    reference 299
Trello
    reference 106

U

Unconditioned Stimulus (UCS) 41
Unity SDK V2
    reference 255
Unity
    assets, importing 184
    assets, setting 184
    basic core concepts, implementing 159
    brainstorming tool, implementing 120
    PlayerPrefs 251
    prototyping tools 147
    quick navigation 159, 160
    reference 152, 267
    user profile system, creating 58

V

W

Z